DAVID W LITWIN

Author of CRE8TVE SUCCESS and Parables & Parallels

MLK2.0

The Steps Needed to make **YOU** the Next Great "World Shaper."

PURE FUSION MEDIA
Oro Valley, AZ

All rights reserved. No part of this publication may be reproduced, stored in a retrieval system, nor transmitted in any form or by any means–for example, electronic, photocopy, recording–without the prior permission of the publisher. The only exception is brief quotations in printed/online reviews.

Copyright © 2017 Pure Fusion Media
All rights reserved

TABLE OF CONTENTS

1 MLK2.0 AND THE POWER OF "WORLD-SHAPING"

2 WORTH - Knowing your value

3 RECALIBRATE - Shedding your external past

4 EDUCATE - Leading through the leadership of others

5 MESSAGE – The intellectual property of the next big thought

6 INCLUSION - Speaking to the masses

7 INCUBATION - Marinating in your world-shaping idea

8 AUDIENCE - What the social landscape looks like

9 PRESENTATION - What is your method and medium of transmission?

10 FOLLOW-THROUGH - Creating "stickability" with your world-shaping idea

11 LEGACY - Shaping this–and future–generations

EPILOGUE: SPARKS – Spring boarding off some of my world-shaping ideas

Chapter 1:
MLK2.0 and the Power of "World-shaping"

Let me start with the first elephant in the room. I'm white. I grew up a in a middle-income household in an all too quaint suburb in Cupertino, California. I went to high school in the 1980s. That's far from the poverty-stricken ghetto or the hate-infused townships of the South in the 1960s. As far as the title of the book, let me be clear that I don't know anyone related to Martin

Luther King Jr. and, apart from his writings and video footage, I have no connection to this great man.

Instead, the title of this book began with a question I kept asking after watching every political argument, every angry protest, every "us vs. them" post on social media: *"Where is this generation's Martin Luther King Jr? There's so much polarization and endless division in our world today. Inside those dividing lines are leaders who speak to their particular groups and tribes, but who, like MLK, is speaking in a way that resonates with all of us?*

Maybe you're asking something similar, at least more today than ever.

When I ask this question, I don't necessarily mean where is a man or woman of the same race and social class as MLK? That may be the case, but the next MLK could be Asian, Indian, Black, White, or any other color or ethnicity. He or she could be rich or poor, impressively educated, or have barely passed high school. That does not, nor should not, matter.

Instead, I hope that you, the reader of this book, develops the character *and generates the impac*t of MLK.

MLK2.0 AND THE POWER OF "WORLD-SHAPING"

Martin Luther King, Jr, literally, *spoke to the masses.* His words transcended social classes. They pushed beyond racial boundaries. He shattered ideological and religious barriers. It didn't matter race, creed, color, or religion. His words communicated into the hearts of *nearly* everyone.

His ideas not only resonated with all classes, ideological biases, and religious convictions, they also *applied to them as well.* You didn't just listen to the man, you inserted his words into your life and it made a positive difference, regardless of who you were or where you came from. He changed more than his generation. He changed history.

History desperately needs another man or woman like MLK.

Today, America appears pulled in two nearly polar opposite directions. That tension is ripping us *all* apart. With 50% believing one way and 50% the other, few voices have the capacity to bring even their own 50% into agreement, let alone 80% to 90% of the populace. We need someone capable of speaking *to, and for, all us* today. Someone whose words relate to us at our core, not just to our personal preferences or chosen ideologies.

Are you seeing people like this on our cable news networks? Do you read about them on entertainment blogs? Are they talking on daytime talk shows? Or are most leaders and influencers speaking to their bases, connecting with their particular tribes?

Although this generation's MLK may not be too evident, thankfully, *it's possible* for a man or woman to garner an even greater level of impact.

With the improvement in broadcast technologies and the rise of social media, now anyone *can* have a voice. This is both incredible and incredibly detrimental. While it allows many the opportunity to get their powerful and positive ideas out quickly to the global world, it also encourages millions of other voices to opine, argue, and assert their beliefs without the research or application to back it up. From biased news networks, to internet blogs, to politically charged Vlogs (Video Blogs), opinion rules the day. Often, the louder and more outlandish the voice of the opinion, the more additional voices, and social followers, it collects.

We also now consume mass quantities of social memes, humorous gifs, and videos that do little more than take up brain mass. I'm not attacking these forms of digital consumption; their rise has given birth to something far greater. For though much of the content of social media may be trivial, the transmission technologies that send the content are incredibly vital and expansive.

Remember the blue/black or white/gold dress internet controversy of 2015? It created a social firestorm, reaching around the world in a single day with hundreds of millions of views, followed by mammoth national/international news coverage. In less than 48 hours, the world voraciously devoured a picture of a dress displayed on a hanger.

In just minutes, the right video, the right thought, or the right candid camera shot can reach the entire world in "the blink of an eye" through the internet. Imagine the global impact of MLK in an age with technologies this powerful? In other words, what if an idea, an, "I had a dream" concept, carried that much *immediate* impact? I believe it's possible.

WHY 2.0?

I titled this book MLK2.0, and not "The Next MLK" because of what we just learned in last page or so. The upgrade in technologies allow for an upgrade in the voice of these new leaders. There's now no limit to the impact that one man or woman can have. That leads to a massive amount of responsibility, as you'll discover in the first few chapters, but it also leads to huge possibilities, ones that should be available to all of us if we change, listen, and humble ourselves to the process.

Instead of focusing on MLK's impact in the past, goal of this book is to shape the world in the future. More specifically, it's about becoming, cultivating, and broadcasting ***your world-shaping idea.***

For I believe with all my heart that you have an inherent idea, placed inside you by a loving Creator, that can impact and transform the world. It's apparent MLK had them. His words are still, or in some cases, even more relevant today.

They just don't belong to MLK.

Thankfully, many people I know have been given world-shaping ideas. As I spend time with others, I've helped them shape and define these ideas. I'm writing this book because I believe that you, too, are destined with *at least one* world-shaping idea.

To understand the difference between a good idea and a world-shaping idea, we need to go back to MLK. Remember, MLK didn't speak to a tribe or faction of humanity; he spoke to *all* of humanity. Your world-shaping idea is bigger than your social circle (but it might start there), and more transcendent than your blog tribe (where most people believe similarly to you). Your world-shaping idea will resonate with the masses, or it's not world-shaping. It will be inclusive, it will be grounded, and it will have lasting impact across social classes, races, religions, and ideological/political biases.

We can certainly say that MLK was a world-shaper. What about you? Am I right in my hypothesis, that you harbor world-shaping ideas hidden at your core as well? I'll never be sure. After all, how could I prove it? I probably don't know you, nor am I connected to your personal history. I have no way to validate your abilities.

That's not the point.

It doesn't matter where you come from, what your social or economic status might be, or how much influence you have or don't have at the moment. If *you were to generate a world-shaping idea*, the broadcast mechanisms to get it out to the masses are available to you today, and like the positivity of Pascal's Wager*, I choose to believe it for you.

More than MLK ever could, you have the capacity to get your voice heard at this precise moment in history. That's obvious and undisputed. Now you just need the right idea to generate MLK's level of impact. *This book is a journey down the path of who you need to be and what you'll need to do to find, incubate, and broadcast that world-shaping idea.* More than the idea, it takes a *certain type of person* to see it actualized.

WHY WORLD "SHAPING?"

Here is one of the reasons I've seen it work in the lives of many whom I know and why I chose the words *"world-shaping."* Many people want to be leaders. Many more want to be famous. Leaders and famous people are ubiquitous in our world. It takes something far different to become a "world-shaper."

I grew up in the church, and in many Christian circles that I frequent there's a thread of thought that People of Faith need to be at the top of the "Mountains of Culture." That "believers" need to lead government, media, education, etc. The aim is to bring God's leaders to the head of the table of a broad range of industries.

As a Bible reading Christian, I've noticed that those in Scripture who retained head leadership, held top political power, failed pretty miserably. King David imploded. Solomon sort of became a hedonistic nihilist. Moses never saw the Promised Land. King Saul failed almost before he began. For most of the Biblical leaders I read about, the outcome wasn't very pretty.

However, there are two men that had very little negative Biblical press in the scriptures: Joseph and Daniel. Both men rose from predominant obscurity. Both men were complete outsiders. Both men never controlled the throne. *They influenced it.* They captured the hearts and minds of the leaders of their societies without being the leaders themselves. They *shaped* culture; they didn't dominate it.

Moreover, they shaped the reasoning and actions of men who didn't even agree with Daniel or Joseph's ideologies or belief systems. Think about it. How often does a Republican senator influence the attitudes of a Democratic leader, or vice versa? How often does a Christian look to the writings of the world's top atheists for insight and inspiration? These two men from the Bible had ideas so powerful and profound that they transcended all biases, socially, religiously, politically, etc. just like MLK.

World-shaping works and manifests because it's not about personal credit. Joseph and Daniel didn't seek the head position, yet they shaped nations. Their goal was the transformation of the culture, not for the culture to worship them. World-shapers don't need credit, though it might happen. They don't need accolades nor awards, but eventually they may receive them.

To become a world-shaper requires change and sacrifice. These ideas don't just come out of nowhere, nor do they manifest fully formed. There are steps. There's a personal path. **You must *become something new* before ever discovering and sharing your new idea.** World-shaping with the wrong intent, or using the wrong timetable, creates an implosion of incredible magnitude.

I wrote this book to purport that there's something better and bigger than fame; more important than entertainment; and more vital than getting 100 likes on your viewpoint on Facebook or your blog on Wordpress. There's nothing wrong with these things. There are just greater, and more needed, inspirations in the world.

MLK2.0 AND THE POWER OF "WORLD-SHAPING"

What are needed are world-shaping ideas. Or, better yet, *your* world-shaping ideas.

Therefore, I'll start with this question. *Are you'lling to make a difference in the world, without anyone knowing that it was you who made it happen?* Can you sit back and listen to others recite the impact of your idea in their lives and never tell them it came from your mind and heart? It's not probable, but it needs to be a possibility for you. It's the foundational gate you must decide to open before walking the steps toward discovering your world-shaping idea.

Once you answer that question, you can begin this adventure, or conversely, you can say no and put this book down. The steps outlined in the next 200 pages take a lot of hard work, dedication, frustration, and, above all, humility. I'm inviting you to potentially journey to a place without personal recognition, but your ideas may influence thousands, even millions, of lives. Like MLK, your world-shaping ideas may change history.

I'm certain that the world needs your world-shaping idea, if you're willing. I know that I need it. MLK transformed history. MLK2.0 will not only do the same, but do so in a matter of years, days, even minutes–not just over decades. So, I hope you've made that first decision, that you'll willingly open the gate and start this journey. Who knows? Perhaps the next big idea that influences my life came from you.

Live inspired.

Chapter 2:
W O R T H:
(Knowing your value)

"We were meant to live for so much more; have we lost ourselves?"
Switchfoot, Meant to Live

As you discovered in the last chapter, I believe you have the opportunity to be more than a leader or just become famous. You have the capacity to be a world-shaper, like MLK. Moreover, I'm confident that you inherently carry a world-shaping idea which could revolutionize humanity, even change history itself, but if you'll ever rise to greatness and *successfully* influence hundreds, thousands, and even millions, **you must first understand that you matter.**

You have worth.

You have immense value.

You are "fearfully and wonderfully made."

It's somewhat easy to *hear* those words, isn't it? Regardless, we often spend our lives, our talents, our treasure, and even our character to get others to recognize our worth.

For most of us, the concept of personal worth and value hasn't reached our soul yet. We attempt to validate our worth rather than rest in it.

The world's systems know this. No, better yet, they capitalize on it. The majority of the things that flow through your eyes or penetrate your ears contain the following statement, "you'll have worth if."

If you buy this sports car.

If you reach this weight.

If you date this type of person.

If you go to this school or get this job.

If you just reach 10,000 subscribers.

Consider this statement:

Another study demonstrated that firms can put consumers into a temporary narcissistic state of mind

with marketing techniques. For example, customers were shown an automobile advertisement with the slogan, "You impress. Like the new Audi A6," that capitalized on their desire for admiration.
http://www.sciencedirect.com/science/article/pii/S00224359150 00834 (The Influence of Trait and State Narcissism on the Uniqueness of Mass-Customized Products)

We use external forces in an attempt to fill a need of the soul. It's big business.

It just isn't healthy.

Consider something like narcissism. Narcissism is not a confidence in one's self; it's a confidence in one's self because of X, Y, and Z (you fill in the blank). Often our worth, or whatever fragment of it we believe in, is built single brick upon brick, growing up toward the sky. It looks like a huge column, but push on it slightly and it topples and crashes.

We allow these marketing forces to represent fallacies. Alcoholic beverage companies sell community and good times to masses of consumers, yet the majority of people who consume alcohol on a daily basis drink alone.

Because for many of us, we need something, anything, to fill the void. We hope that keeping busy remedies the need for introspection, but can you sit in a room and reflect for five minutes in complete silence? Not even meditate (that's still doing something), but just relax, take deep breaths, and enjoy the stillness of nothing but you in the moment?

To quote the movie *The Help*, can you look in the mirror and say, *"You is kind. You is smart. You is important?"*

Contentment is a foundational trait of a world-shaper. Are you content just being you?

THE NEED FOR (AND DISRUPTION OF) CONTENTMENT

Contentment exposes advertising tactics, eliminates the need for external validation, makes excessive alcohol and narcotic usage irrelevant. It puts social media on the backburner for face to face conversations. When we rest in who we are, at our core, we've the capacity to build out. We become an external conduit through our internal development.

We radiate.

Have you ever noticed people content in who they are, despite their quirks, their flaws and their social or financial position? For some, this creates a desire for emulation. We want to be like them. For others, it generates a dangerous sense of uncomfortable agitation.

Going back to *The Help* for a second, remember the young and uncomfortable outsider, Celia Foote, who marries into the world of the Southern socialites? She was truly friendly, truly genuine. She knew who she was, despite her differences, her flaws, and her rapidly manifested insecurities.

What was she met with?

Disdain. Derision. Gossip. Malice.

Many people have a hard time keeping up appearances around the contented. They tear the contented down, place them on their level, then shove them further downward. For those trying to live lives of contentment, the naysaying voices pile up, leading to a lonely state of existence for the contented.

Thankfully, like the Matrix, others around you *want* to be released from their sub surface, un-contented exterior shells. Individuals and groups desperate to hear your clarion call of contentment and come running, shackles falling off as they race toward you. That makes up for all the naysayers you interact with along the way.

It's better to be content in who you are, rise to great things, and face a little persecution than be miserable (or oblivious) in self-doubt, worry, and false narcissism and never reach your full potential. Humanity may not recognize it, but they are missing out on the words you're too beaten down to speak.

How can you grow more content? Ultimately, we find contentment by recognizing the scope of our worth.

WHERE TRUE WORTH COMES FROM

To fully understand your worth, you must understand where true worth comes from. Worth arises from many things: your parents or family, your educational teachers, a coach, or a caring friend or neighbor, but at the core, your worth is first found in your Creator. Now, for some reading this book, that statement might shut down the conversation. Many today don't believe in any god, let alone the God of the Bible. Moreover, the number of individuals asserting

He still exists seems to be slipping downward every decade.

Many today claim that existence is just random happenstance. You're little more than lucky mud, here for a whisper of a moment before vanishing back into the cold, unforgiving nothingness when you pass. Science seems to validate it, many of our most expressive leaders and stars believe it, naturalistic philosophers attempt to create ethics and inspiration around this idea of naturalistic origins. I don't wish to argue their beliefs and attitudes. I don't need to dismantle their preconceptions.

To understand and grasp true worth, you must understand why *God's account* of you matters. Many religions claim a diety or dieties made humanity. From multiple gods, to stardust, to alien spawns, most religions and belief systems provide a creation account for humans, but the God of the Bible is the only one who states we were made in *the image of the One who created us.*

That changes everything. Imagine you were to create a beautiful painting. It's so beautiful, in fact, that it draws public attention. Your painting goes up for auction, with asking prices rising into the millions. Just before the gavel comes down on the final bid, you come back and purchase that painting with the highest bid, then, in the presence of everyone, you douse it with turpentine and set the painting ablaze. What would be the reaction?

Sure, people might think you were a little nuts, even get a little angry, but soon they would go back to their lives, forget the event, and move on. Imagine you were to treat your children with the same callous treatment. If you were to harm them, what would be the reaction? Public hatred? Vilification? Incarceration? Naturally. That attitude is inherent in us, but why?

The difference in impact and perception is that your children are made in your image. They reflect the character, traits, personalities and visage of their parents. How we treat our children is a direct reflection on how we view ourselves. If they do well, it brings them, and us, glory and favor. We're inexorably tied to our children, because they're not just our creations, they're made in our image. Their value and our value are connected.

That's how your Creator sees you. You're a direct reflection of Him, a mirror, so to speak, on this earth. The wonder of the stars and galaxies don't look like

Him, the ocean and its power doesn't look like Him, Mt Everest doesn't look like Him. You do. The best of you reflects His character, love, and enthusiasm.

You're worth more than anything that has ever been created, invented, or manifested. This can become a beacon by which to navigate, a landmark you can return to again and again when fear, doubt, and mistrust take up real estate in your mind and soul. True worth produces true contentment, because it's tied to nothing that you can control. It simply just is a part of you.

WHY DOES WORTH MATTER IN WORLD-SHAPING?

Worth is incredibly vital for a world-shaper, because you must be as content in obscurity as you are in fame and elevated opportunity.

Undeniably the most contented Man to walk the face of the Earth, Jesus, once said:

"No one puts new wine into old wineskins. If he does, he will burst the skin and spoil the wine."

Although He was referring to something in particular, in this moment, we can mine this metaphor for far deeper meaning. Think about your world-shaping idea, your success, your fame, your legacy, your contribution to the world as the wine. You can use that wine to brighten the lives of everyone you come in contact with. To heal. To create laughter and wellbeing. To build a sense of belonging among individuals. To transform their realties. All that great stuff wine can do (well, mostly in moderation).

To pour out that wine, you need a vessel, a container, metaphorically, what is that container?

It's you.

Better yet, it's what makes up you.

It's your character, your value, your strength. What's more important, the wine or the wineskin? They both work in concert, and therein lies the rub.

If you believe in Providence (and I hope you do), it makes logical sense you won't Providentially receive the wine unless you, as a wineskin, are capable of containing it. Like Jack Nicholson shouted in *A Few Good Men*, if you aren't content in yourself now, "You can't handle the Vision!" Or the fame. Or the accolades. Or the success.

Why?

Without becoming the right wineskin, you'll self-implode at some point along the way. We see this happen every day in the public square. Some implode early and become forgettable quickly. Others experience meteoric rises, only to then burst into flames, showering burning fragments all over their unsuspecting followers.

Sadly, some fail to grasp that they've imploded. They keep blissfully going on, never recognizing the aftermath on their fan bases, networks nor tribes.

Consider the seventeen-year-old pop star sensation who dresses and acts a little too provocatively. It works for her. She's got bodyguards and 24-hour supervision and security, but let's say a fifteen-year-old super fan figures she can dress and act the same way. She goes to a high school party with a bunch of testosterone-filled senior classmen. The combination of alcohol, ego, and unchecked libido form a dangerous and sexually illegal concoction. Two years later, the pop star cuts a new hit record and the super fan graduates high school with a three-year-old, after sending three young men to prison for rape charges. Her emotional and physical scars never fully heal, despite the new lyrics of her now nineteen-year-old music idol.

CONNECTING THE DOTS

What did we just learn? Did you catch it? *The wine isn't about you!* It's about all those you touch and influence. Implode during the process and everyone in your influential circle faces the aftermath. Each with their own undetermined consequences, shaped by their own walks in life.

To become an MLK2.0, you must see the world this way. You're interconnected with everyone around you. Our actions, however quick or misguided, produce real-world consequences on others in ways impossible imagine. The more influential we are, the more potential consequences we unleash.

WHEN 'RESISTANCE' GIVES THE GREEN LIGHT

Steven Pressfield, in the incredible book *The War of Art*, talks about all the negative forces against you using the term "Resistance." I love the term, so I'll use it here.

Resistance attempts to stop you from doing great things in the world. It seeks to frustrate and destroy all positive or transformative change on, and for, others. It attempts to blockade you on all sides and at all costs.

It drops all barriers and smooths out the road for a person without the inner character and/or conscious worth to handle the spotlight. It yearns to see the implosion. It feeds on it. The wisest man to ever live, Solomon, was plagued with a question:

Why do the righteous suffer and the wicked prosper?

The answer?

Resistance doesn't care who gets hurt when you get there. Money, fame, and celebrity is just a means to an end for Resistance's end goal of destructive aftermath.

I've already shown this on previous pages, but you have to see it *tactically*. If you're going to do great things, if you're going to be an MLK2.0, you have to see the illusion, the Matrix, first. You can't just be the most influential person in the Matrix. We already have that. Those people are ubiquitous. As you'll see in Chapter 5, amass sway over their tribes, their collective groups, their fans, but it often goes no further. Your Matrix can be your political party, your religious affiliation, your educational bias, your music genre.

You can become a big fish in a small pond. Or you can show people a new pond. That's what MLK did.

Think about it:

"I have a dream!"

Was metaphorically saying, "I have seen a new pond, and let's all swim in it together."

Wow, MLK was the Twentieth Century's NEO.

I don't believe we've one yet for the Twenty First Century.

Maybe that'll be you.

Believe in yourself. Better yet, believe in the One who believed in you first. You already have a cheering section, one with more power and opportunity than you could ever achieve on your own, let alone imagine. Connect to that now may be difficult, and that's okay, but know that your world-shaping idea manifests out of how you're shaped first. The journey isn't easy, there's a lot we need to remove first, but knowing your worth lights the path through the next step in the process.

CHAPTER 3
RECALIBRATE
(Shedding Your External Past)

In the last chapter, you discovered you have immense worth. Capturing and embracing that reality is the beginning of the path toward becoming the next great world-shaper, to becoming an MLK2.0.

First, you must scrape off a potential lifetime of negative sludge fighting to stamp out your world-shaping ability and your world-shaping idea.

I could say it's like scraping barnacles off a luxury yacht, but a better metaphor exists. First, let's go back to scripture for a second and quote a rather fascinating verse.

"Do not be conformed to this world, but be transformed by the renewing of your mind."

Stripping out the spiritual implication, the last chapter displayed, in vivid color, the hollow and damaging "conformity" of this world. We must step away from the current Matrix-like systems to find true contentment to prepare ourselves for the amazing journey ahead.

There's an even more powerful word in this scriptural passage: "renewing."

Notice that this passage didn't say "make your mind new," but instead said, "*renew* your mind." What's the difference?

Inherency.

THE BETTER METAPHOR

Stay up late on any given night, and you'll discover that most lower budget cable networks give their least viewed time slots to a little thing called "the infomercial." A product sales-pitch disguised in the form of a thirty-minute entertainment special, infomercials offer inventors and companies the opportunity to display the wonder of their products through real-time, real-world situations. In the 1990s, one particular infomercial opened with the host and the product creator taking a visit to the local auto junkyard in hope of finding a vehicle coated in weather oxidation and rust.

The chosen vehicle was an eyesore, having been left to rot in the junkyard, far from its previous owner's memory, abandoned, discarded, and devalued. The harsh treatment of the weather and the elements had left what appeared to be irreparable damage on nearly every portion of the vehicle's surface.

That was only *the beginning of the show*. Once the product's creator applied his special wax-like compound to the damaged paint surface, the original brilliance and color of the vehicle started to shine through once again. Soon, what had been destined for scrap and removed from remembrance appeared just as pristine as it had on the showroom floor. The creator simply used his revolutionary product to bring the vehicle back to its original and intended beauty.

In other words, the creator "renewed" the vehicle back to its intended and inherent beauty. Taking it back to the passage that started the chapter, when you "renew" your mind, you're once again returning it to its *intended* state. You're not doing something revolutionary, but, according to (and working through) Providence, you reignite something that was always there. That's pretty liberating.

It takes away the striving to achieve something that appears impossible and recognizes that I'm walking into what I was always designed to be.

Can you get there *without* Providence? I'll answer by quoting one of the most well-known cartoon quotes in history.

"Now you know, and knowing is half the battle."

Just knowing about this inherency is pretty transformative, but remember, it's only *half* the battle.

Let's leave that there and talk about the oxidation in the metaphor. We discussed around it in the last chapter. It has many forms. I defined the negative *external* forces with Pressfield's term of "Resistance," but personally, for you and me, it *internally* originates from another place.

Ego.

EGO AND THE FALL OF MAN

It was Freud who gave it a name, but its origin incubated much further in the past. Assuming you've heard the Christian explanation of the beginning of the world, you know that God first created the world in perfection and intimate relationship. Everything he made was "good." He then created two beings, Adam and Eve, to cultivate the good world he had created. It wasn't long before these two were manipulated and tricked into going against God, eating from the single tree on the entire global landscape God had prohibited. God came back to spend the afternoon with His created couple, only to find them hiding in fear, then God asked them about their fear and what they had been up to.

" But the LORD God called to the man, "Where are you?" He answered, "I heard you in the garden, and I was afraid because I was naked, so I hid."

And he said, "Who told you that you were naked? Have you eaten from the tree that I commanded you not to eat from?" The man said, "The woman you put here with me—she gave me some fruit from the tree, and I ate it."

Genesis 3: 9-12 NIV

Before that moment, there was nothing in humanity that needed to prove itself, to validate its own worth, to excuse its flaws, but the first thing Adam did after being challenged by God was to blame shift.

Ego, in that moment, was born.

Ego is always in constant self-preservation and self-satisfaction mode. It just doesn't have your best interests in mind.

We sleep around and open ourselves up to diseases, depression, and even infertility, often due to our need for the validation we failed to receive from our parents or other relationships. We take drugs to deaden the lack of self worth and loss of value we feel, or we assume we're invincible to its inevitable outcomes.

We often, especially in our younger years, get drunk to prove we're socially acceptable. We overeat because we attempt to fill a void that Ego continues to drill deeper into. We create dictatorships based on our own despotic grandiosity.

Ego is the driver in the list in the previous two paragraphs. Ego is *fueled* on the externals. It, like fire, is never satisfied. There's always a prettier woman, a bigger house, a nicer car for us to revalidate our worth through. In other words, Ego and Contentment are sworn enemies.

Ego rushes us head-first into dangerous situations, fuels thoughts in our head of getting even or worse, pushes us beyond natural and healthy limits to achieve X, Y, or Z. It hijacks Worth. Distorts it, then it attacks us when we can't achieve it. My favorite singer songwriter, Jack Johnson, wrote of what he called "the Shadow." These lyrics can easily reference Ego.

"Your shadow walks faster than you, do you really think your immune to it, do you think that you're not alone?... It will defeat you, then teach you to get back up, after it takes away all that you've learned to love."

While Contentment may be Ego's enemy, its blood brother is Addiction. Addiction often starts with actions caused by the Ego. We engage in dangerous activities to validate our identities or stifle our lack of worth. Eventually, however, Ego gives its power *over* to

Addiction. Once it *"takes away all that you've learned to love,"* Ego's job is done.

Let's get strategic for a moment. Addiction is the most damaging cog in the machine of life. Even over death. With something as dramatic as death, those affected by the deceased individual can grieve and move forward, but Addiction holds the addict, and everyone in the addict's relational, financial, and social circle, hostage throughout the lifecycle of his or her addiction.

There's real danger here, and it's of our own making. Organizations and marketing systems develop mechanisms and strategies to stoke Ego's fire without recognizing Ego's far more permanent, if not sinister goal of addiction. Corporations collect profits off the Ego-driven actions of the populace, not recognizing (nor turning a blind eye to) the aftermath left on the citizenry.

When you see the strategic power and danger of Ego, you can start recalibrating against it. Thankfully, there are telltale warning signs to see how much market share Ego has accumulated in your life.

HOW DO YOU HANDLE OFFENSE?

One of the easiest ways to determine if Ego has its shackles around you, is to assess how you act after someone offends you. It doesn't matter what the circumstance: talking back against you, sarcasm, gossip, even cutting you off on the road, how do you respond? Do you feel anger rise in your heart till you can taste it in your throat?

Do you spend every waking moment from then forward figuring out how to get them back, to repay them for how they treated you? Or do you lash back out in the immediate moment, letting civility drift away as you yell or curse your way into a better state of being once again?

That's Ego manifesting in the moment. It's shaped by you, but it has its own personality, its own trigger points. Have you gotten way too angry in a moment, then later said, "How could I have acted that way?" TV crime dramas are replete with stories where the unchecked Ego led to tragic and/or criminal circumstances.

In our age of global and immediate social critique, you must get offense under control. As Taylor Swift wrote, *"Haters gonna hate, hate, hate."* What happens when they turn their sights on you? Can you handle the criticism, no matter how unfair nor distorted it might be?

Mishandling offense is the first and quickest form of implosion. Many people hit this first stage and give up. It's too much to handle the damage to the Ego. Some of the greatest thoughts have never been spoken, written, nor sung because of offense. Resistance laughs. Ego feels vindicated. The world suffers.

HOW DO YOU HANDLE PRAISE?

The second way Ego claws into you is through your reaction to praise or accolades. Do you feel the need to brag to others after someone gives you a compliment? Are your social media posts filled with self-praise? Do you attempt to show nothing but the best of yourself at all costs?

How important is it to get praise in line? One of the most powerful global leaders in history said this:

"The measure of a man is not found in how he handles offense, but how he handles praise." – Abraham Lincoln

Why? Because Ego lives for more and more praise. Like offense, praise will push you past normal, healthy limits. Think about how we often post our bodies up on social media. Do we position the camera or remove clothing to get the optimal angle or view of our physiques in hope of criticism or valid critique?

No! We want praise! We want people to say "we're hot!" so we do whatever we can to achieve it. We buy certain cars, purchase certain houses, even date certain people because we want others to admire us. We max out credit cards and even create falsified, inauthentic relationships for external affirmation. It's often dangerous when it interacts with the real world.

Kim Kardashian was known for her opulence and skin-exposing photography so much that she published a book simply of her body selfies. She could often be found flaunting her possessions, including jewelry costing well into the millions of dollars. Was she showing her possessions and her bodily assets on social media to underscore the frivolity of glamour and decadence? No, she wanted affirmation, acceptance, and praise, just like most of the rest of us.

The problem was that these images were also studied by those with nefarious interests in mind. On a fashion trip to Paris, she was tied up and robbed at gunpoint. The ten million dollar ring, flashed on social media earlier that day, was snatched from her hotel room. Thankfully, all they took were her possessions.

This isn't to say that Kim warranted these actions, but that Ego doesn't remain unchecked nor isolated to the individual displaying it. Without keeping Ego in check, when it comes to our need for praise, we open ourselves up to external circumstances over which we've little control.

EGO, PRAISE, AND WORLD-SHAPING IDEAS

When the need for praise dominates our lives, it often drowns out the voices speaking world-shaping ideas into our hearts and minds. Why? Because our oratory and thought energies are focused on ourselves.

Years before I learned this lesson, I used to love to go on first dates. On a first date I could become anyone necessary, based on the woman I was seeing that night. Did I need to be a bad boy, a charmer, or a gentleman? Whatever I determined the woman needed at the time, I would morph into that evening.

Until a good friend of mine, a wise man, sat me down. He had watched my behavior for over a year. We met over coffee, during which I was probably staring and flirting with the women in the booth just over his shoulder. He looked at me and said, "You must be exhausted!"

I looked back at him. "What do you mean?" I inquired. He then spoke words I'll remember for the rest of my life. "You must be tired of staying in your head all the time, trying to figure out who you need to be and what you need to say to get affirmation from women you probably don't even care to see again. In an effort to stroke your Ego, you have no time for anything valuable in your life or in your thoughts."

He was wise. That was provoking. Thankfully, I listened. I could not have written this book without that and many other powerful moments with other wise people.

HOW DO YOU HANDLE ADDICTION PRODUCING ACTIONS?

Ego pushes us to unhealthy, dangerous, and deadly limits. Nowhere is that more apparent than in our embrace of Addiction-Producing Actions, or APAs. Addiction-Producing Actions are any actions with the capacity to produce physical or psychological addiction. Some of these actions are governmentally illegal. For example, we know that smoking meth is a jailable offense.

Other actions are not so obvious. As our society has "progressed," we've lifted restrictions on many APAs, from marijuana use to gambling to prostitution.

Most of these actions, even in their infancy, have powerful neurological consequences. That's a problem and a great danger. These actions just don't feel good to you; they feel good to your body and your brain. Once the body captures a sensation, it wants it again and again. The body itself will push you beyond your own limits to reengage in the sensation. In other words, the fight you have against addiction, is a fight against your own body. It's not a fight against your willpower.

Ego wants you to frequent these APAs, to keep you in the cycle of addiction. Like praise and offense, it draws your focus elsewhere. Ego also knows it will force all the others in your life, to some large or small degree, to focus elsewhere as well. Like I stated previously, Addiction ensnares *everyone* around the addict, relationally, vocationally, financially, socially, and psychologically. It's one of Ego's greatest strategies and most potent outcomes.

Remember Jack Johnson's lyric:

"It will defeat you, then teach you to get back up"?

Ego says:

"You're not going to get addicted."

"You can handle it."

"Don't you want to be cool like everyone else?"

"Will you *always* be a loser?"

Then it morphs:

"You'll never get out of this."

"You'll always be a loser."

"Just give up."

Ego will utilize any means necessary, say whatever needs to be said, in your head or through the voices of others, to get you caught in Addiction's perpetual cycle of destruction.

DISTANCING YOURSELF FROM EGO

As you diminish Ego in your life, its decibel level will grow more distant. You'll have the capacity to hear new and different voices. I hope you don't mind me going back to scripture often, but it contains metaphorical insights I can't capture elsewhere, so I'll continue to use it for your benefit, not merely to proselytize.

In the Bible, the enemy of humanity is metaphorically defined as a "roaring lion." Elsewhere in Scripture, God's voice is described as a "still, small voice." If both are present and neither's nature changes, how do you hear a still small voice over a roaring lion? The answer?

Proximity.

If the lion is fifty feet away, he can roar all he wants, but his roar is deafened by the distance. Through the lack of his frequency, the still small voice comes in loud and clear.

You have to agree with Ego to allow it to ransack your life. You need to know how it operates and what it sounds like to push back against it. Or, better yet, replace it. This has its roots in neuroscientific reality. Any time you think on an action or thought, your brain builds pathways to that line of thinking. The more you dwell on it, the stronger you make the pathway. How do you starve a neurological pathway? Create a new pathway through a new course of action or thought and dwell on it for a while. The longer you focus on the new pathway, the more the older pathway diminishes. Focus on Contentment and the positive, and Ego will begin to lose market share in your thoughts and actions.

EGO IS NOT DRIVE!

One thing that must be made clear is that *Ego is not Drive*. Drive can motivate us to do great things, scale new heights, reach unfathomable goals. Drive is by nature positive. Ego is inherently and intentionally destructive. How can you tell which is in control in your life? The answer is found in what you have to sacrifice for Drive or Ego to attain your goal.

Ego will always demand *unhealthy sacrifices*. Drive will produce positive sacrifices, even if they appear costly in the process. A person who gets in optimal physical shape through Drive will cut out things in life that may appear beneficial, but aren't necessary, such as large amounts of food or time spent watching television. Ego will have them sacrifice their bodies (such as bulimia or anorexia), or push them beyond their limits (such as repeated plastic surgeries). Once a person has reached his or her goal, Drive will motivate others to do the same. Ego will keep all the praise and results of the fitness (overt sexuality, narcissism, etc.) internally focused.

If you're uncertain of whether you're being motivated by Drive or Ego, ask yourself, what will I have to sacrifice to gain the result I'm hoping for? That will force Ego out of its covert hiding spot and allow Drive to take its rightful place.

EGO: IN MEMORIAM

Let me quickly sum up the three areas of Ego and how to address and eliminate them in your life:

Offense: Forgive

Praise: Deflect and Redirect out to the others

Addiction-Producing Actions: Don't allow yourself to get caught up in their damaging cycles. Be vulnerable with others about your struggles. Avoid.

For the rest of this book I'll help you build new pathways, to see new vision for your life and for the lives of humanity in hope that Ego's pull becomes irrelevant in your life. If you can see the vision and act upon it, you can release hundreds, thousands, even millions from Ego's grip in their own lives. That should be a path worth continuing.

CHAPTER 4
E D U C A T E
(Leading Through the Leadership of Others)

"I'm what I'm because of who we all are."
Martin Luther King Jr.

I will continue to shout throughout this book that I believe that you have, inherently developed inside of you, a thought or an idea that *could* change the world. In this chapter I'll be clear that this world-shaping thought or idea will never come from just you.

One of the things science has begun to uncover is that everything in nature operates in a form of "synthesis." What happens over here affects what happens over there. I recently watched a trailer for a film where two surfers studied years of weather patterns to ascertain where the biggest waves would be all over the world during each month of the year. They spent the next year riding the biggest waves on the globe because they studied nature's predictable *patterns.*

In the first book I wrote, yet never published, I postulated and displayed how we are all interconnected. Each of us, across society, across nations, across the world, and even across history is intricately bonded to the rest of humanity not just because of our actions, but because of the consequences (or outcomes) of our actions. What happened fifty years ago through the single conscious choice of a corporation's CEO in a country on the other side of the world may have had a real impact on your existence today. Sure, it's true that technologies shape us across societies and history, but the outcomes of our seemingly (or claimed to be) benign actions have perhaps had even more impact.

For example, cell phones are critical for our lives today. We use them in every area of function. That's technology, but the cellular towers that fuel our need for this enhanced function may actually cause some of us *less* function in the future. A Stage 4 Cancer patient living under a cellular tower in a lower income housing development is now effected by the rest of us and our need for greater function, and so is everyone whom cancer patient can never create touch points with again, from family members to work environments to areas of commerce. This level of connectedness, like nature's "synthesis" occurs around us all of the time. Again, to quote Jack Johnson, let's:

"take a time lapse and look at it <u>backwards."</u> (Never Know)

This level of synthesis is also generated at the thought, or idea, level. **Each of us is a collection of the thoughts, insights, ideas and ramblings of others. We're shaped by what we see, hear, and consider.** When you talk with your best friend, you're listening to all of their previous listening. What they have heard and adopted or heard and discarded.

You can understand this reality, or you can use it. Many people now do. People often muse at Oprah's success, abilities, and financial status, but if you really listen, you'll discover that she simply reads and applies what she learns from others. She's an amalgam of her past listening. Her success is, in part, based on applying the successes and strategies of others with even greater success and wisdom.

This means you can be smarter than the smartest people in history! Why? Because those men and women had their era and the previous eras to build their insights. You, however, have all of the time *since* those individuals to collect new information, new insights, and new inspirations. You can combine it all to produce something even more powerful than those men and women ever could.

In a moment I'll describe why, at this point in history, your ability to generate a world-shaping idea has been sent into the stratosphere, but first let's state the obvious.

If all of this is available to you, you must educate yourself. You must become a student of other's past insights so that you can contribute something new to the synthesis.

The lie is that you don't have the ability to contribute to the world, but remember, world-shaping ideas aren't coming just from you. They're coming from all of those incredible people before you. You may simply add one thought, one sentence, or even one wor to their ideas and create something more profound than they could have considered.

The first question you have to ask yourself is: "Do I really want to make that kind of difference in the lives of others?

Ego says no.

"Really," you might say, "wouldn't Ego want that?" Ego wants the recognition, but it doesn't want to make a difference. We can say it this way:

For Ego, the byproduct of recognition may be making a difference.

For world-shapers, for those becoming an MLK2.0, the byproduct of making a difference may be recognition.

This is why you must *recalibrate* before you educate. You'll never accept other people's words to the level necessary for world-shaping if you aren't in the process of crucifying Ego.

As you remove yourself from your own equation, you'll better process and consider the words of others. You'll discover how their ideas pertain to *your* life, but you'll also begin to ponder and marinate in how their words can impact others around you.

When you see an inspirational film, do you keep it to yourself? No, you share! You want to pass on the experience to others.

Why don't we often do the same when it comes to the *words of others*? I think it lies in the impact of the medium. I've often told people that:

Movies and television happen at us.

Music happens to us.

Books (or words) happen *through us*.

We process, in our own way and through our own lenses, the words spoken to us, or the words on a page. Ego is the great deflector, but a person who has removed power from Ego is often like a sponge. There's a hunger inside him and her. There's a thirst for more knowledge, wisdom, and insight. Remember half time during those intermural soccer games in your youth? Exhausted and thirsty, the coach often handed out orange slices (in the days before Gatorade). In that thirsty and exhausted state, what did you do? You sucked that orange down to the rind. That's how a world-shaper sees the words of others. What can I learn from those words and what can I pass on to the masses?

WHY ARE SOME PEOPLE SO SINGLE-SIDED, BORING, <u>AND</u> JUDGMENTAL?

Have you ever been around people who have little depth? It's as if they're stuck on autopilot, cruising through life and relationships based on a single way of thinking. I just heard a story about a man whose mother came out as a gay woman in the 1980s when he was about six or seven years old. As he described the situation to the interviewer he said, *"Where we lived was a pretty religious area so, you know, there was a lot of judgment."* The tragedy of the story was that it was presupposed that the interviewer could relate to that statement. Religious people equal judgmentalism. Why?

I've been thinking about this recently because I've been listening to podcasts with a few freely-accepting spiritual type speakers, and I continue to notice how little they offend guests who often think differently than they do. What I realized was it has to do with this idea of Education. They can celebrate the differences of their guests because they can value their thought patterns, even if they don't subscribe to their premises. I don't mean that most religious people don't educate themselves, but their education tends to stay in a certain domain, spoken by others who stay in that certain domain, spoken by yet others who stayed in that certain domain before them.

In other words, many religious people are reading the words or hearing the sermons from a microcosm of the possible voices that are speaking both currently and (sadly) historically. They don't have the breadth and range of voices across a broad expanse of ideas and considerations, and in so doing, there's little new to discover. They all sound similar, because they're all getting their Education from the same 100 people who got their education from the last (or even same) 100 people.

This is not to say that they don't know their scriptures. They may be masters of the text, but they often fail to apply those scriptures into all aspects of life, and all ideas of thought. C.S. Lewis once said, "I believe in *God like* I believe in the *sun*, not because I can see it, but because of it all things are seen."

Lewis was one of the last great religious authors unafraid to study a panoply of other writings and engage other philosophies. In fact, it was his deep fascination and knowledge of mythology that led to a lifelong friendship with JRR Tolkien which led him to embrace theism, then Christianity. You must be willing to engage in other ideas, to read and understand varied and opposing viewpoints, so that you can add more depth to words and ideas that you may never agree with.

Remember the idea of Ego and Offense? To many, words offend. To a world-shaper, even offensive words can cause growth. Nothing offends because there's nothing to attack. There's only opportunity.

Is world-shaping a big enough opportunity for you? I believe that if you're reading this book, it might be for you. I wanted to give you a big goal, or you won't let Drive take the reigns in your life. There are just too many enjoyable outside factors.

Imagine if I told you that if you spent the next six months training all day, cutting out all television, most of your social time, and overhauling your diet, that you might place in the top 100 in your local 5K race? Not much of an incentive, is it? Instead, what if I said that if you did those exact same things, you would win the Boston Marathon and receive all the accolades and opportunities that go with it? Did that influence a new decision?

What changed?

The opportunity behind the exercise.

That leads to why I believe that, at this point in history, I can write a book about world-shaping *to the masses*, and not the fortunate few.

YOUR EDUCATIVE MEDIUM: THE INTERNET

For many, the internet is a form of entertainment. In many ways, it produces completely *new forms* of entertainment. It has opened up the global populace to entertainment in ways that were impossible even fifteen years ago. Justin Beiber and many other artists and celebrities were discovered out of obscurity through sites like YouTube, SnapChat, Facebook, and Tumblr.

Of course, you know that.

For world-shapers, however, the internet is the number one resource to discover, cultivate and validate ideas that can change the world. People, sometimes ruled by Ego and a desire for recognition, share everything on the internet. If you really think about it, college is often a moot point today, apart from skill-based degrees such as medicine. Not only is the full curriculum from any university available at a finger click, but also, with a few rare exceptions, everything about a topic has been uploaded to the internet.

The internet allows you to hit every angle of an idea or concept to make it your own or discover everything its author thought or considered. This is especially true with religious study. When people pick up the Bible and read, say, the King James version, the original Greek and Hebrew words the transcribers read, and the definitions they then provided in the text are based on the culture of that day. For example, at the time of the writing of the KJV Bible, Religion was often about control and power, and most of the language in the text reflected that mindset. It's all about context.

With the internet, we don't need to take context for granted; we can research it ourselves. What was happening at that time in history? What was the geography of the land? Who else was an influencer in that day? What was the demographic of the people in the area?

A hundred years ago you would have to have had relationships with a historian, a language expert, a topographer, and a sociologist. Thirty years ago, if you understood the Dewey Decimal system and had hundreds of hours to research, you may have discovered *some* of that information. Today, you can learn all of that information in less time than it takes to defrost a turkey, and it comes packaged with all of the personal commentary (good and bad) from a myriad of other expert (and amateur) voices. Then take that information and start connecting the dots. Take an idea from here and combine it with a finding from other there and you'll produce something new. If you can see the synthesis in the world, your possibilities for combinations of wisdom and insight are endless.

The internet is a powerful tool for uncovering information, but when it's combined with *Inspiration*, it becomes a forceful and positive weapon.

WHERE DOES INSPIRATION COME FROM?

In the incredibly romantic and insightful film *Always*, a young hot shot flyboy named Pete Sandich (played by Richard Dreyfus) lives the dangerous life of an aerial forest-fire fighter. He's a consummate risk-taker and a vibrant lover of another aerialist, named Dorinda (played by Holly Hunter). His love for her runs deep, but his passion for flying and risk-taking run even deeper. On a particularly dangerous fire-fighting run, Pete dives a little too close to the fire line. Engulfed in the flames, his plane's engines fail and his plane bursts into a massive fire ball.

Seconds later, Pete wakes up in the middle of a now smoldering forest and, of all things, he's in the process of getting a haircut by a mysterious woman named Hap, played by the quintessentially radiant Audrey Hepburn. They dialog about the moment prior and how close he had come to, wait, he shouldn't be in the middle of the forest getting a haircut. He should be, dead?

In fact, he is. His daredevil, carefree attitude got him killed, but that wasn't the end of the story. Instead, Pete learns that he still has a role to play on Earth. Once he comes to grip with the situation, and she finishes his haircut ("Keep the sideburns," Pete requests), she shows him a vision from out of the past. In an open field, a small prop plane soars in the air above them. Pete livens up.

```
            Pete:
               (excited)
        Hey, look! I did my first solo
   in one of those!
```

Hap:
That's right.

Pete:
I did that! Boy, was I nervous! But you want to know a funny thing? Once I got up there, I felt like a veteran.
I couldn't do anything wrong.
I flew that plane like Fats Waller flies his piano…

Hap:
You think you did that by yourself?

Pete:
There was nobody else up there with me.

Hap:
There was, Pete. There was someone like you. Behind him was someone else. Maybe someone who learned what he learned on a motorized box kite. And you knew

> that, though you had a different word for it.
>
> Pete:
> I did? What word?
>
> Hap:
> It's what fliers and piano players...
> ...and everyone else count on. They reach for it. They pray for it. And often, just when they need it most, they get it.
> It's breathed into them.
> It's what the word means.
> Spiritus.
> The divine breath. Inspiration. Inspiration.
> And now it's your turn to give it back.
> That's how the whole thing works…

There are endless ideas as to where inspiration comes from. Eastern religions often claim it comes from a person's ancient ancestors. Some modern mystics claim it comes from the "Universe." Stephen Pressfield attributes it to the "Muses."

I believe in Providential inspiration, but from wherever it originates, an inspirational thought or idea needs weight and backing to become world-shaping.

Inspiration is truly a single seed, and it's often first watered through motivated, energized research.

When I use the term *research*, I know many of us groan and revert back to our college courses, remembering the crushing weight of our 20+ page research papers and the misery that ensued until we finally turned that thing in.

Research backed by Inspiration is life-changing. You're building up a deeper understanding around a thought that came out of nowhere. With every new affirming bit of information, you'll revel and marvel. Educate hard and reap the rewards. To quote Pablo Picasso:

"Inspiration exists, but it has to find us working."

APPLYING EDUCATION

Let's get practical at the end of the chapter. How do we start the Educative process? Here are four techniques utilizing the Internet. I recommend applying these techniques in succession.

1. Can't Read a Book? Start by Reading Quotes.

Maybe you don't have time to read a book at this point in your life. I get that. We're all busier than we'd like to be, but you can easily read quotes. Reading quotes is a great way to extract the divine nuggets out of an individual's psyche. It's like *microwaving* your education. Your steak will never taste quite as good as throwing it onto the grill, but it's not bad tasting, and it will sustain you.

Start with reading quotes by people you agree with or that you find interesting. This will inspire you, which is a great way to start the Educative process, then move on to those with opposing viewpoints to help develop *nuance and empathy*, which we'll discuss later.

Find times in the day to share these quotes with others. Often, some of my greatest ideas and insights have come out of moments sharing a quote with someone else, only to discover something new about my idea as we process together.

Practically, one of the best quote sites online is *brainyquote.com* which is tagged and referenced, so you can search an individual or an idea easily. The hyperlink references allow you to go and read more about that quote to gain further insights into their thought processes.

2. Research Ideas

As you collect ideas, you'll want to explore deeper. Use the internet to search out more on a subject. I've discovered new treasure troves of insights and strategies regarding faith, the Law and the way life was intended to be lived through my study of neuroscience. I never read even a single paper about the field during high school or college.

Research with the internal thought that you may discover something new because you're seeing the idea or concept from a new perspective, at a new time.

Create a Microsoft Word file and throw down notes and copy link addresses. You can go back over the ideas at any later date and build on the idea further. Keep a journal (for moments away from the computer), but there's only so much room on the paper. Microsoft Word allows you to cut, paste, edit, and revise ubiquitously. Since Word files are relatively small, you can save a new file every time you edit. That way you can always go back to ideas that you may have discarded in the past. Ask good critical questions and let that drive your research.

3. Connect Dots

Here's where you'll differ from others. There are many who assert that we live in a random, chaotic universe. X is X, and Y is Y, but X in relation to Y is rarely considered. Because if there are correlations across multiple domains, it questions the randomness of existence.

You can choose to live that way, but it will hinder your world-shaping idea. Instead, start researching on the internet with the premise that some random finding over here can radically impact and merge with some random finding over there. Remember how I said that you can be smarter than anyone in previous time periods? With the internet, you can connect dots that simply couldn't have been discovered without this repository rich technology.

I believe that Inspiration can guide you to search in ways that cause connectivity. Be willing to listen. You can read other people's commentaries, but don't be married to them. Chart your own path through the ideas, and don't let anyone dissuade you from making correlations they couldn't find themselves.

4. Test Theories Online

As you accumulate research and further your Education, you can start testing those thoughts and receiving other's opinions. We'll talk about this a great deal on future pages, but why not start by asking questions on Facebook? Most people *like* to be heard on social media (Ego often gets its fix through Facebook). It's an easy way to get seed-sized ideas to blossom into conceptual plants and trees that may start to nourish others.

Make sure you ask questions and not assert ideas or (God forbid) opinions. Questions are more disarming, and you'll get broader opinions on your idea by keeping the conversation open. Try to steer the dialog away from one train of thought and certainly don't let your friendship base turn on each other. Moderate well and you just may start to cultivate that next big idea.

Here are a few of my most recent questions:

Do Americans swear as much as Hollywood thinks they do?

Are you asking the right questions to further the paths of your friends?

Have you ever heard something so inspirational and profound that it changed your entire life? Would you share it please?

I've used the answers given by friends to shape some of my thoughts in this book and other ideas I'm postulating at the present time. Let your friendship community help you shape an idea that just might change that community in the future. Remember again, your world-shaping idea is never going to come just from you!

GOING RADICAL

I'm not recommending that you do the following, but it worked for me. In the early 2,000s I felt called to do what I'll call a "media fast." For what turned out to be two years, I shut down all forms of broadcast entertainment media (music, TV, movies, and video games). To replace the 6 – 8.1 hours day that I had freed up, I delved into about seventy books, read scriptures about three hours a day, and meditated often.

I would create "takeaways" from each book I read, underlined and had written notes across. Those were translated to Microsoft Word files which could be referenced later. I used the internet to ask and answer questions that I felt "inspired" to research.

Within six months, people started asking me where I had received my philosophy degree, *which I didn't have*. I became sought after for my insights and began to speak often. Since that time, I've written five books, lectured at leadership conferences, and I now consult with powerful leaders on a daily basis.

Again, this "media fasting" exercise may be extreme, but I'm certain I couldn't have written this book or experienced these opportunities without that history.

Discover for yourself what may be radical and decide if it's worth letting Drive make the sacrifices to achieve your world-shaping goals.

CHAPTER 5
MESSAGE
(Cultivating the Intellectual Property of the Next Big Thought)

"Almost always, the creative dedicated minority has made the world better."
Martin Luther King, Jr.

Often when I get together with a pastor or some other spiritual leader, the first question I ask him or her is, *What's the one thing that you believe God has called you to share with the world?* All too frequently, they don't have a definitive answer to the question. That shocks me. If you're going to lead a congregation, be an influencer of multiple hearts and minds, I believe God is going to give you a precise and unique message to share with your congregation, your community and, potentially, the world.

No two snowflakes are precisely alike. A piece of fruit from one tree will taste slightly different from another identical piece of fruit from a tree in a different area. Wine takes on the flavor characteristics of the soil its grapes are planted on, and I believe that your great world-shaping idea will be a unique thought or concept that no one else has ever been given because of your unique soil. No one else has ever been quite like you. Therefore, your world-shaping idea will stem from three major areas that formulate your unique soil:

Your History
Your Passions
Your Convictions

These three areas not only form your worldview, but will also help you discover and define your world-shaping idea. Let's break down each of these in further detail.

YOUR HISTORY: (GIVE ME SOME BACKSTORY)

I left California in 1998 to pursue a career in film writing in Nashville, Tennessee. Yes, everyone in both regions thought I was nuts. Why leave California, the movie capital of the world, to head to a place where, at the time, few films were being written, let alone produced? For me, it was a calling, so I went. Film writing never fully manifested into a career, but what I learned as a struggling script writer has been essential in my writing, speaking, and communications to this day.

One of those critical understandings is in the development of a backstory. Any character you see on screen, if the script is well developed, has a fully thought out and rich backstory. The backstory is the written documentation of what constituted the character's past life. It can be anywhere from two to twenty pages or more. It's never shown on screen, but the backstory helps shape everything a character says, acts upon, and accomplishes during the filmed storyline. Often the richer the unseen backstory, the more depth to the character we see on screen.

Each of us has a unique history. For most, it's easy to see that history as happenstance. Some of that happenstance may be enjoyable, some depressing and, for others, tragic. Some of us have a history of our own making; others have had our pasts delegated to us through the actions of others.

As we're most likely the center of our own universes, we often fail to see any bigger picture to our history. It simply just is.

I have a friend who used to be a womanizer, a scammer and a schemer. He knew how to manipulate situations (and women) to his own advantage. When he became a Christ follower, he was deeply saddened by his past exploits. That's understandable, but the Biblical scripture says that, *"God works all things together for our good."* As we became friends, I told him that all of that "backstory" would help him moving forward as he shared and lived out his new testimony to the world. That dynamism and former scheming ability has now been sanctified. It's still in there, but it's now used in a different way. Instead of scamming others, he now *influences* others, speaking and consulting with top leaders in key businesses on how to develop powerful business experiences for their customer bases and how to live vital and fulfilled lives.

We don't need to run from our past history, but instead look at it from a ten-thousand-foot view, and sometimes from a whole different perspective, and ask what can I use from my past *to further my future?* Some of that past may be tragic, and it may be hard to see the silver lining in it at all, but there's the possibility that even out of the embers of tragedy, new birth and revelation can manifest.

MESSAGE: CULTIVATING THE INTELLECTUAL…

Going back to our last chapter, education is also included in your history. For some, that may be affirming or, for others, deflating, but remember, education is a never ceasing phenomenon. You can start today and become ten times smarter through a two hour inspired internet research session than you were even a single day before. Live by this Chinese proverb:

"The best time to plant a tree was twenty years ago. The second best time is now."

YOUR PASSIONS: (WHAT'S MY MOTIVATION?)

I love watching cooking competitions on the *Food Network*. Sure, it's fun to watch the challenge of it, but I love the stories. I enjoy hearing great chefs recite how they grew up listening to their parents' desires for their lives, then became doctors, lawyers, or business leaders, but something inside them burned for more until they found cooking. They then gave up all the success, prestige, and revenue of the past to enroll in cooking school, work as a line cook, then make their way up to Sous Chef or Executive Chef. They went from having a job to loving what they do every moment of every day.

These chefs are now walking in their passions.

I wish we learned this earlier in our lives. I think that the lower education models have become outdated. High school offers courses to the masses that *may* prepare students for college, but offer only a few slim "electives" to allow students time (an hour and a half at best) to venture into areas of interest. My recommendation is that every sophomore in high school is given a personality and leadership profile test. Using the findings of those tests, the school crafts a custom program for each student for the next three years. How much richer and more sustainable would education become for students if they cultivated their inherent passions during their most formative years?

Like our unique backstories, each of us has been given unique passions. Connecting with your passions produces powerful results.

For many of us, we've been so beaten down vocationally that we've forgotten that we even have passions, let alone can communicate what they are. Therefore, let me give you a quick question to answer. It may help steer you in the right passionate direction.

If you were to take over Tim Cook's job at Apple, what is the first thing you would do as the new CEO?

Perhaps you might say, "I would change the way the iPhone looks. It's too angular and not intuitive enough." Your passion may be for interior or mechanical design or a career in an art field. Or, you could say, "I would change their commercials. They've lost their edge." You might be skilled in advertising or marketing. Maybe you would suggest, "I would pay the employees a sizable amount more per paycheck. After all, the company can certainly afford it." You might be skilled in finance, human resources, and certainly a field with empathy like medicine. There are hundreds of other possible answers because each of us is unique. Find your answer, then consider what it might mean for you.

Practically, you might want to go online and take a personality and/or leadership test like Strength Finder or DISC to discover more about how you're wired in your passions. It's never too late to make those discoveries. Those discoveries will provide a road map to passions that may have remained dormant for years.

Begin to marinate in those passions. Consider where they could lead in your life.

Your passions will drive you forward, but your convictions will cause you to act.

YOUR CONVICTIONS: (WHAT WILL I FIGHT FOR?):

"There comes a time when one must take a position that's neither safe, nor politic, nor popular, but he must take it because conscience tells him it's right."

Martin Luther King Jr., A Testament of Hope: The Essential Writings and Speeches

Your conscience is a powerful guide, but unlike inspiration it's often shaped by experience. I'm often surprised when two people with polar opposite viewpoints can argue with such deep conviction on a subject or belief.

Convictions are good, but they can betray you, because they often come from an internal, historical source. We'll discuss this in far more detail in coming chapters, but to be led by a conviction, one must ascertain whether or not that conviction truly benefits humanity.

Not a portion of humanity, but *humanity as a whole*.

We've plenty of people speaking to portions of humanity. What set MLK apart from the myriad of voices since is that he spoke to *all of humanity*.

This isn't to say that everyone will be in agreement with your convictions. Remember, other people have their own convictions fueled by their past experiences.

How do you ascertain if your conviction is truly of benefit to humanity? Going back to the last chapter, you have to do research. You have to know your conviction inside and out, at every level, and through every form of thought and disagreement, all while being objectively honest in your research. Why? As I mentioned, not everyone will agree with your position. If you can see and understand your position through their eyes, you'll have a better chance of helping them see through yours.

I never said it would be easy. Remember you're looking for *world-shaping* ideas. They come with a cost and a lot of effort.

There's an ancient proverb that reads, "Do not answer a fool according to his folly; answer a fool as his folly deserves." Answering a fool according to his folly is speaking with conviction about a subject that you know little about. This is especially true with religious convictions. Christians, specifically, often live through the former bumper sticker, "God said it, I believe it, and that settles it." While I understand their intent, that mindset is truly answering a fool according to his folly. There's no backing behind the conviction other than, "My Daddy told me so, that's why!" Did it work in the schoolyard growing up? It certainly isn't going to work today with all of the research, case studies, and scientific data available to both you and those with *opposing viewpoints.*

I can argue intelligently against legalizing most narcotics. It's a conviction of mine, but I don't argue based on morality or a "Daddy said not to" religious frame of reference. I have the neuroscience, the legal history, the social data, and the biological findings to prove it. If taken on their own, each of these findings is potent. Connecting the dots shows a far deeper reality, one that I've discovered and shaped through Providential Inspiration.

My well-shaped worldview, combined with the knowledge I've discovered from the world, has allowed me to understand that the "high" of narcotics *is not the intent of narcotics*. The "intent" of narcotics, apart from even the financial goals of its manufacturers and dealers, is to destroy your life and (especially) the lives of those around you. The "high" is merely the mechanism with enough physiological to tempt you into engaging in narcotics in the first place.

You may disagree, but I have the findings, the insights, and the data to back up everything spoken in the last paragraph. Furthermore, my insights point back to many words spoken in the Biblical scriptures, but I never have to speak religiously, quote a single verse nor argue anything from a moral perspective.

My conviction, in this case, has been grounded in reality, not theology nor solely in my personal history. I've written this book, because I'm certain that you'll be able to accomplish similar feats in areas that you're convicted in, but remember, don't coat your insights with your own frame of reference nor simply cite those who agree with your premises. Keep them in mind, but you must be able to validate your convictions with not only neutral data, but with even *opposing viewpoints*.

This means that, for many of you, your most passionate convictions may be proven to be null and void. I'm sorry about that, but this world has too many people now arguing with "fools according to their folly." It's ugly and unproductive. It may garner some media attention, but it's not going to positively nor profoundly impact the world.

As your history, passion, and convictions collide, and as you consider your Providential makeup, your world-shaping idea will most likely be birthed out of a question, not an answer. Remember, *humility is one of the keys to becoming a world-shaper*. You have to be willing to accept that there's much you don't know. What you do know, and what you educate and inspire yourself in, will help lead you to the right questions. You can jump start the process by reading authors and listening to other leaders and asking, *What are they missing? What more could be discovered here?* Most likely, you're going to add to their previous learnings, but remember, this is the key to your world-shaping idea:

You're going to say something new, or you're going to say something old in a new way.

Your message, to be truly Inspired and world-shaping, won't be a regurgitation of someone else's thoughts. Those thoughts will influence your idea, but they won't plagiarize it. There are too many people all saying the same thing, all agreeing with each other. World-shapers are different. MLK coined the term "creative-extremists." You'll be on the cutting edge of thought and future actions. It will most assuredly draw resistance and much skepticism, but if you've cultivated your ideas, grounded them in objective reality, and spoken them in a fresh language, you'll have all the tools and confidence to see your ideas through.

CHAPTER 6
INCLUSION
(Speaking to the Masses)

"People fail to get along because they fear each other; they fear each other because they don't know each other; they don't know each other because they have not communicated with each other."
Martin Luther King, Jr

The main attribute that delineated MLK from most every speaker and leader to follow, and the reason that I chose to write this book, is that MLK *spoke to everyone.* He transcended political lines. He transcended economic status. He pushed beyond religious and ideological biases. His words resonated in the heart of humanity, not just a select, like-minded few.

If you're going to be a world-shaper, if your thoughts are going to make a true difference, you must have the same aim. We've had enough bias, enough partisan talking points to cover now till eternity. It seems to be getting worse rather than better.

When I first started writing this book, I tried to avoid much of the religious content in my presentation. I'm not afraid of my faith; instead, I'm worried about the language and attitudes of many of those claiming to be religious. There's often little empathy in much of the religious language of today. There's certainly a lot of "us against them" vernacular coming from religious leaders. I didn't want a reader's supposed world-shaping idea to be judgmental, biased, or exclusive, but as I worked through this book, I realized that so many of the requirements found herein come from recognizing your Creator and engaging in His processes of transformation and inspiration.

That doesn't change my intent nor downplay the need for inclusion.

The world, cognizant or not, is desperate for words that are **empathetic, nuanced,** and **inclusive**. To help you delve into this mindset even deeper, we're going to unpack each of these attributes in more detail.

EMPATHY

As much as we love to watch and read stories, we often forget that every person on the planet has a story of his or her own. Forgetting those stories often opens us up to judge. Judgment stems from a shortsided, immediate view of the world. Judgment categorizes people in the moment. It fails to acknowledge a person's past, the parts of the story that comprise the person whose actions, beliefs, or preferences we judge.

Religious people often appear to be the most judgmental. They compare. They label. They look down upon. Ironically, the leader of the most subscribed to religious system on the planet, Jesus, said metaphorically,

> *"Or how can you say to your brother, `Let me take the speck out of your eye,' and behold, the log is in your own eye? You hypocrite, first take the log out of your own eye, and then you'll see clearly to take the speck out of your brother's eye."*

Matthew 7:4-5 NASB

Why do you think this Man chose to use the word "speck" for something small, but "log" for something large? If you're describing something "large," why not reference a boulder or a mountain, something that's actually big? Why a log?

Unlike a boulder or other large inanimate object that just "is" large, a log is organic. It starts from something small. A seed. Slowly, with both time and the right amount of watering, the seed grows and germinates, sprouting into a solid and permanent tree. Eventually the tree would be cut down, and the final result of an initial seed is the log.

Like a log, the person we are at any moment is the culmination of that historical germination process in our own lives. Sometimes we carry a log of our own making. Other times, through tragic circumstances, our log has been made for us, but every log started as a seed. Jesus is not saying that there's no perceived speck in your brother's eye; instead, each and every one of us has a log, and a seed, in our eyes. The question is, which object are you going to focus on?

Judgment sees people for their logs; empathy recognizes and acknowledges seeds.

Going back to the last chapter, we would say that empathy cares about a character's backstory. The seed of a person's backstory makes up the story character of the moment. Empathy not only recognizes the backstory; it enters the story through the other person's eyes. An empathetic person sees the person holistically, understanding how the past formulates the present. He or she also strives to help the individual create a better future, not for himself nor herself, but because that individual is a glorious part of the human race.

Judgment sees logs. It often turns man against man. Empathy recognizes seeds and creates concern between men. Empathy requires us to relate, not merely to be in relationship. I can be in your PTA, book club, office building, or church group and by default be in relationship with you, yet never relate to your backstory.

SYMPATHY IS NOT EMPATHY

People often confuse sympathy with empathy. Sympathy creates a standard, measures others by that standard, then self-righteously grieves for the person missing that standard. Do you see how religion can foster this mindset? In the highly successful and inspiring book, *The War of Art*, Stephen Pressfield compares fundamentalism and art, stating, "There is no such thing as fundamentalist art." We could reinterpret and say that fundamentalism and the search for human meaning are mutually exclusive. Judgment is often bred in fundamentalism, the "God said it, I believe it period" mindset. We can then judge a person based on a moral standard that we may or may not be living up to ourselves. Empathy is developed when we recognize that not only does everyone have a backstory, but also that everyone has value. Sympathy is far more bent toward fundamentalism than empathy. Sympathy is feeling at someone. Empathy is feeling with someone.

Your world-shaping idea must come with this kind of weight attached. Who's going to be impacted? More important, *how* will they be impacted? You may shape new ideas or you may rigorously dismantle old paradigms, but you must do so with grace and concern.

A world-shaping idea will never attack. It will inspire, encourage, and challenge. It doesn't mean that you won't get attacked because of your idea. Remember, people's convictions fuel their attitudes and often their actions. People may passionately disagree with what you say, but they should never be able to attack *how* it's presented.

NUANCE

Your world-shaping idea will most likely start as a question. As I've stated, that question will need to be researched. It has to researched from every angle, dissected from every viewpoint. Your goal is not to prove a point; it's to change and shape the mindset of humanity. Therefore, you must engage in all facets of what it means to be human. Nuance says, "There are things I don't know." Assertion *destroys* nuance.

I came out of a rather judgmental church in the buckle of the Bible Belt. Many in the church not only believed that they had the answer for those in the rest of the world, but also even for those churches that were "less enlightened." This was not only saddening, it's the exact opposite of nuance.

Like a diamond, there are many sides to a single idea or thought making up the whole jewel. Assertion flattens out the shape and dampens the brilliance of the stone. Watch any two-sided political conversation on Fox News or MSNBC. Most of the time one side will speak with assertion, using his or her talking points.

What happens when the other side attacks or dismantles their argument? The original speaker will often get louder, flustered and, in many cases, belligerent.

There are, however, ways to be more certain while still having nuance: study your ideas in and through objective domains.

WHERE OBJECTIVITY COMES FROM

Everything people say is subjective. Everything people write is subjective. It's, at some point and in some way, opinion is based in some worldview or another. Many Christians believe in the Inerrancy of their scriptures. That everything stated in the Bible is true and accurate. I don't mean to argue this, but if the Bible is your sole form of reference, despite its supposed "sola scriptura" Truth or not – it's still subjective, at least to those who don't subscribe to similar beliefs. It's a closed loop, with little power outside of the loop itself. To become an objective idea or belief, the idea must transcend the domain of original discovery.

The objective standards to ground most arguments are actually found in our biology. When

Shakespeare said, "If you prick us, do we not bleed?" he was affirming this reality. When you cut yourself, your body begins the clotting process to heal the area. It didn't ask your opinion. It didn't happen based on your worldview. It clotted because that's what your biology is designed to do. Your body is not subjective; it's objective. In part, because it's not really under your control (that's a world-shaping idea that has allowed me to speak to many leaders in medicine).

When you can uncover how something impacts the body, in whatever arena, neuroscience, genetics, oxidated stress, etc, you are no longer arguing your insights through a subjective worldview.

Illegal drug users can argue the benefits of narcotics for them. But they can't argue the science of what occurs in the body and brain when they are using. Going back to the political news channels again, it's okay if someone gets belligerent when arguing against your biological findings – to him or her, you're attacking their fundamental, but flawed personal belief. Regardless, do so with the utmost empathy.

Statistical social data is also nearly objective. For example, if 25% of those living within a half a mile of a Cell tower contract cancer, that presents a fairly objective discovery, but there are a myriad of factors that go into any statistic. You'll have to be nuanced and accommodating when researching social statistics. Many statistics found on the internet are based on furthering the author's personal agendas, which can cause the author to pick and choose their findings to match their preconceived ideas. You'll have to go deeper than that. You never want to be the one who gets belligerent when someone dismantles your poorly considered assertion!

    Another way to add objective weight to an idea is to focus on outcome, not bemoan a person nor a society's original actions. Actions are subjective. They're based on the ideology, belief, or even whims of its actor. I can act any way that I want, at any moment. I just can't control the outcome of my actions. Outcomes are not based in ideology; they are based on the natural, factual world.

    If I smoke for ten years and get lung cancer, I don't have existentialist lung cancer, or post-modern lung cancer, or deistic lung cancer. I have cancer. Outcome doesn't care what you believe about the world, it's objective, and it's undetermined. It isn't based on your desired timetable either. *We've little control of how, what, or when outcome occurs.*

People can argue all day (and they do) about the validity of their actions, but they can't argue outcomes. You can't tell a doctor, "I don't feel like I have cancer today," or "cancer doesn't gel with my beliefs."

Most important, when you focus on objective outcome over subjective actions, you show care for the individual or culture suffering through the outcomes. For far too long, too many factions in our society have viciously attacked people for their actions instead of lovingly exposing, addressing, and remedying outcomes they never asked for. That changes with you and your world-shaping idea.

INCLUSION

Despite what's happening in our present-day culture, your world-shaping idea must never create nor encourage polarization. Granted, it *may* be controversial for certain, but if your idea takes an "us against them" mindset or attempts to lord an idea over another group, *it's the wrong idea.*

You may gain some sway over a "tribe," but it won't go much further. I think the "tribe" mindset has ruined social media, damaged social interaction, and fueled narcissism. It allowed people to form factional ideas that developed fans while isolating other groups. Instead of engaging on a macro level interconnected dialog as humans, we segment off by our passions, convictions, and skillsets. Ironic, isn't it? Those things that shape your identity, as we've discussed, can fracture your inclusive participation in the human race.

People like to surround themselves with others who agree with them. It's easy. It doesn't take a lot of work nor sacrifice. It's also fearful and weak. Sorry to be so blunt, but if you only surround yourself with those who believe the way you do, how do you really know you are right? If we're to get raw and honest, we often stay in our tribes because we're afraid we might not be right, that we might not have all the answers.

My wife spends some of her free time on Instagram. She loves posting photos and reading other people's stories. She has social media relationships with varied people across the world, many with views and ideologies that she will probably never agree with. Recently, she came to me and said, "You know, it's sad that many of the women I follow assert that they're strong introverts and don't like to be around people, but they still love to interact and opine to their followers online." Nothing against the introverted, but for those who, online, have stated that they don't like to interact with people, Instagram becomes a narcissistic crutch. Translation, "I don't like people in person. I just like the emotional rush of having followers."

Since we're speaking of social media, let's go a bit further and discuss Facebook. **Facebook is not a tribe centric medium**. People often attempt to use Facebook to get out their political or religious biases, but Facebook is (or should be) made up of your high school best friend you haven't seen in 20 years, the workmate you've never gone to lunch with, the guy or girl you met at a concert or bar one night who thought you were interesting, ad infinitum. Your Facebook friends should be a huge collection of disparate viewpoints and ideas, because your interactions and connections are simply that diverse. At least, I hope that's the case.

When I left that church I spoke of previously, I noticed that most every friend I had from that church had exactly the same Facebook friendship list as everyone else from that church, apart from a few different family members. Though it appears that you're being loyal to your "spiritual family" it is the epitome of fear, if not control. Sadly, most others eventually unfriend those types of people because, when they present opposing viewpoints, they're attacked by the group or "family" as a collective whole.

If you're going to be a world-shaper, stop asserting your political and religious bias on Facebook immediately. Those words you post now will be brought up in the future by those who seek to take you down. You'll also quickly discover your lack of empathy and nuance after you stop.

In addition, refrain from using tribe centric or religious vernacular when on social media. It only works with your tribe. It comes off elitist and separatist to everyone else. Learn to speak in language that everyone can relate with. This isn't to diffuse your beliefs, but to show how your beliefs transcend their own biases and standards.

Remember, Jesus said about His system, His "Good News," to *"taste and see that the Lord is good."* He didn't say "hear and learn" nor "accuse and judge." That *should* silence many of the voices coming out of Christendom today.

I've discovered that I can argue any point I've researched, especially on supposed "moral" issues, without ever having to quote a single scriptural chapter or verse, nor quote anything or anyone that comes out of the Biblical Worldview. I can say something that may offend someone, but it will never point back to what I believe. It doesn't need to. I've discovered that what I believe correlates with reality, not a particular ideological viewpoint.

Here's the important distinction. What I've come to believe validates my worldview view, but it doesn't solely originate from it. I can use my worldview as a "lens" by which to look at the world, but I use the world's language, in all its facets, as my transmission mechanism.

That took ten years of hard study to understand, and those last two paragraphs might be too far-fetched to believe at this time. As you craft and hone your world-shaping idea, I believe it will have more significance to you.

Your idea is designed to shape the world, not segment nor fracture it. If you want followers, likes, or social accolades by creating an exclusionary tribe, please put this book down now. I didn't write it so you could become popular. I wrote this book because we, the human race, need your world-shaping idea. By starting your empathetic, nuanced and inclusive journey today, you'll begin to the incubate your world-shaping idea for the future.

Practice these three traits starting today and you'll discover more "power" than you've ever known. It's just a different and more wondrous form of power.

THE MOST POWERFUL PERSON IN THE ROOM

There are two main ways to be recognized as the most powerful person in a room. The first is to speak in such a lofty and authoritative way that everyone in the room succumbs to your superior intellect and commanding presence. The second is to inspire, challenge, and encourage others in the room so they leave the room more powerful than they were before they walked in.

The first way is fairly easy, but it's elusive and laborious. At any time, someone else might step up to the plate, challenge our prowess, and put us in our place. More often than not, power plays are a rouse. All

INCLUSION: SPEAKING TO THE MASSES

the patronizing speech is merely a cover-up for our own insecurities.

The second way to be recognized is far more rewarding and intentional. It stems from the recognition that you do have something to say to the world. Your focus is on giving that information away to others rather than steering the credit toward yourself. Each moment you have the capacity to build someone else up or exalt yourself and tear someone else down. The issue becomes who or what takes precedence in your life: your own sense of identity or the value and enrichment of others? There are obviously times to look out for number one, but remember in those moments, you already know what you know, it does you little good to use it to your advantage. At the end of the day that's ego talking, and it does little to improve *your* life.

By being intentional and attempting to build others up, you must delve into their conversations and listen more than you speak. That way when the powerful moments present themselves, you're ready to offer whatever you have to share with the world. Each one of us is powerful in our own way but we all have the capacity to share something that will benefit others, even if it's to help others learn from our mistakes.

Remember, we're about seeing the seed, not the log, in someone else.

There's nothing more rewarding than to hear someone say, "You can't believe what someone told me. It changed my life," only to smile and know they failed to realize I was the one who shared the idea. The reward is not rooted in the recognition, but in the fact that you were able to change someone's life.

Two ways to be recognized as powerful: the first may offer some egotistical satisfaction, but in the end little is remembered and others leave the room deflated and discouraged (if not slightly disgusted). The second usually gets less fanfare, but you can rest comfortably at the end of the night knowing that the little difference you made in someone's life may just change us all.

Your world-shaping idea will also come attached with a history of countless powerful mini moments, as you'll discover in the next chapter.

CHAPTER 7
INCUBATION
(Marinating in Your World-shaping Idea)

"If I cannot do great things, I can do small things in a great way."
Martin Luther King Jr.

As I referenced in the last chapter, your world-shaping idea will be like a refreshing fruit affixed to a beautiful tree with strong limbs and deep roots. The metaphorical point?

The tree matters even more than the fruit.

After moving from Nashville, TN, my wife tried keeping up gardening in Arizona. The ground in Arizona is basically concrete, so we constructed a ten inch raised bed in an area about 4 x 12 feet, filled it with soil and plant food, and planted our seeds.

Quickly, sprouts came up. Within weeks, we had some fairly tall plants. We were excited to soon be sampling some robust and juicy tomatoes and plump squash. What we got were tiny little tomatoes and less than three inch squash.

We had set up the requirements for planting, but we hadn't set the soil to handle the time and depth needed for optimal growth. I pretty much had one tasty BLT and the harvest was over!

An ancient proverb reads that the *"mouth of the wise, will often remain silent."* Why? After all, he or she is a wise person. He or she will usually have something important to say, but the wise realize there may not be enough weight around the concept yet to truly make the right impact.

INCUBATION: MARINATING IN YOUR WORLD...

Remember, you're going after a "World-shaping" idea. You have to think and act like Atlas, holding up the entire world on his shoulders. He doesn't look like the cartoon character Dilbert, does he? He has a body that was shaped and honed through time, dedication, and hard work. Like a jewel, you must continue to refine, carve, and polish your idea until it shines with such brilliance that it illuminates all of us.

In Arizona, the ground we failed to till well enough wasn't sustainable for the right growth. Your world-shaping idea will likely come with a lengthy incubation process. Don't waste that time; find small ways to maximize the time. Nature itself backs that up.

Everything starts from a literal or metaphorical seed. Did you know that the term 'sperm' in most every language is the same word as seed? All of nature works through seeds and incubation. Even culinary experts talk about the time necessary to "develop deep flavor" in their dishes. World-shaping ideas work the same way. Time builds strength and stability to your idea.

There are three areas that will serve during the incubation process: meditation, personal application, and small social release.

MEDITATION

To help incubate your world-shaping idea, you must think about it often. When I say meditation, I don't mean to sit in a dark room and say "Om," though many subscribe to it. For you, simply empty your mind so you can more clearly consider your ideas. Consider what you've been through to discover it, then marvel in that process. Think about every way someone is going to receive what you're going to say.

Scripture references meditation using the term "Mastication." Granted, it's a big word, but the term is most recognized on a farm. Unlike humans, when a cow eats something, it has to pass through four stomach chambers. Each passing takes time, and with each passing, the cow digests a little more of the sustenance it consumed. That's what you'll do. Meditate on your idea for a while, thinking about it in one way, then come back to it and consider it from a different angle.

Don't be afraid to stop at any time during the process and do more research. Inspiration is often birthed out of silence and direct focus. Always keep a journal with you. That way, you can immediately put pen to paper and capture the idea, then transcribe those thoughts into your Microsoft Word files.

Don't just meditate. *Live an intentional, meditative life.* New mystics refer to this as "mindfulness." I love the term, though I personally don't fully subscribe to their applications. Regardless, be "mindful" in every moment of how your world-shaping idea impacts the life you live and the lives of those you interact with.

This requires you to live in the *now*.

Keep asking more questions than you have the answers for. Read more often than you watch television or YouTube. Avoid mind-numbing distractions when you can. Visit the outdoors. Go camping or rent a cabin. Disconnect from the surface noise and you'll already be in a more meditative state.

As you meditate on your idea, it will start to grow and germinate. Don't be afraid if it takes on a new life or radically deviates from your first thoughts. I've built a framework of ideas in my own life, but I can also discover new facets of thoughts I had adopted and grounded years ago. This is especially true when I continue to speak with others. A world-shaper is always looking for fresh inspiration, and even fresher *application,* so don't be afraid to share and listen.

PERSONAL APPLICATION

The first person you'll begin to test out your world-shaping idea on *is you*.

Years ago, I was in a high-level business course in California. At a particular point in the course, we studied a book entitled The *Tree of Knowledge*, by Humberto R. Maturana and Francisco Varela. This book was hyper-complex, dealing with concepts such as "ontogenic structural-pair coupling" and other confusing distinctions. None of those in my study group, including myself, had any idea what the author was talking about.

Instead of futilely reading the same sentences over and over, I began personally applying the words into my life. Soon, even though I was one of the youngest in the course, I became the class expert on the book. I applied the principals *until* I understood them, then I could illuminate others with what I had applied, not simply read.

You are your best guinea pig, because you come to your ideas with the least amount of skepticism. Despite how much your friends and family love you, they aren't going to fully adopt your idea until you're 100% certain of it yourself. Obviously, if your arena is a new understanding on the strategies of narcotics, like I mentioned, you aren't going to 'shoot up' to prove a point, but consider how your idea affects you and practice what you can. Read and apply the books on your idea. Go deeper than the writings themselves. Write your own conclusions to the books you read.

One of the most profound thinkers in technology and social dynamics for the last fifty years was an NYU professor named Neil Postman. From books like *Amusing Ourselves to Death* and *Technopoly,* this "wise man" prophetically uncovered where our society has headed and the dangers attached to a wholesale love of entertainment and technology, but with all that insight, Postman himself stated, "I'm terrible at offering practical advice." He could "see" the problems, but he couldn't offer many solutions.

Maybe you can. That may be part of your world-shaping idea: to be able to conclude what others can only purport.

As you become a student of your idea first you'll gain the weight and depth to start presenting that idea to the world.

SMALL SOCIAL RELEASE

Remember, I said *"Start."* Once you've successfully applied your world-shaping idea to your own life, it doesn't mean that the masses are ready to accept it. Share your idea with a *limited few*. Let's get scriptural again and discuss a formula that seemed to work for the God of the Universe: The Three, Twelve and Seventy-Two strategy.

Jesus, when he walked on the earth, had a group he called his "disciples." They were an intentional faction, but there was an order to the group. First, even in his close knit group of twelve, he had a core three men who contained his closest confidants. With these three, Jesus shared pretty much everything. He put his full weight on their shoulders. They were the ones he could trust the most.

You're allowed to solicit the same number of three (maybe less, but not more) in both your family and your friendship circles. Not all of your family are going to subscribe to your world-shaping idea at first. Choose the three (or less) closest people you trust and begin to share your ideas with them, then choose three (or less) of your friends and do the same. Don't simply exclaim, "I have this great new idea!" Ask them questions, covertly communicate to allow them to consider their actions or recognize your new way of thinking, then see how those questions and thoughts start to impact their lives. Keep your world-shaping idea within this net until everyone in the group has been impacted by your idea, and they even start regurgitating your ideas to others.

After you have seen see impact with the Three, you can reach out to the Twelve. The Twelve are those you know have your back, but you probably wouldn't share your deepest secrets with. Start asking them the same questions bestowed on the core three. Ask them to consider reading a paragraph or two of your thoughts. Get them to respond to your social media polls first, to get the pump primed. Maybe set up a book club or group that you facilitate to help you process your ideas. Speak in inspiring tones and be inclusive. Remember, you want lots of viewpoints to be recognized and considered.

Since many of the Twelve will probably know each other, it should keep the conversations from turning angry and biased, and becoming harder to control. It will probably also help those twelve build stronger bonds amongst each other.

Once the Twelve have become ambassadors of your ideas, it's time to share the idea with the Seventy-Two.

The Seventy-Two are people who you have more than just a social media connection with. You know they also have your back, but you may not talk to them quite as often as the Twelve. Many of the Seventy-Two may not subscribe to your personal beliefs or ideology. *(Note: If every one of the Seventy-Two shares the same ideology or political preference as you, you probably aren't ready with your world-shaping idea yet.)*

With this group, you want to keep your ideas closer to the vest. Instead of blurting out your revelations, think of ways they can apply your thoughts in their lives. Email works well for this group. Perhaps you send them a few (or more than a few) page e-book and ask them to offer any advice. Maybe you call them on the phone and discuss a topic or news article around your idea, then offer your thoughts during the conversation.

You'll want to be more careful with the Seventy-Two, because not all of them will support you like the Twelve and certainly not like the Three. Even people in our close circles can unintentionally tear us down, and cause us to shrink back from our world-shaping ideas. The Three and the Twelve will serve a fuel to your fire when a few of the Seventy-Two attempt to extinguish a bit of the flame. The stronger the blaze, the less likely they are to snuff it out.

Too often people get great ideas, but skip the incubation process and jump right to the Seventy-Two, or more catastrophically, to the whole of social media. The anonymity of social media leads to far more skepticism than support. Like I stated previously, when you're ready to reach social media status, be sure to start with questions and not assertions.

As you see impact with the Seventy-Two, you'll be ready to venture out further. The next chapter outlines the six types of audiences you'll encounter when you start sharing your well incubated, tested, and refined idea out into the world.

CHAPTER 8
AUDIENCE
(What the Social Landscape will look like)

"If I cannot do great things, I can do small things in a great way."
Martin Luther King Jr.

You've now marinated in your world-shaping idea for a while. You've applied it to your own life and tested it on your Three, Twelve, and Seventy-Two with powerful and positive results. It's time to get your idea out into the world. Before I run through the type of people you'll meet as you share your world-shaping idea, let me give you a little encouragement.

There's an ancient proverb that reads:

"Do you see a man skilled in his work, he will serve before kings, he will serve before obscure men."

When this was written four or so millennia ago, the goal was for you to hone your craft with such precision that you received the rare opportunity to stand before a king and present your world-shaping ideas. Today, all you need for a king or queen of a nation to discover your world-shaping ideas through a YouTube video, blog, Instagram post, or SnapChat is a computer, tablet, smart phone, or any other digital device. With your world-shaping idea and little technological effort, you have the capacity to change the course of an entire nation from a king's Google search or a Facebook share from one of his high school buddies. You can change the thoughts of a leader of an entire society in a micro-moment.

That should be encouraging and validate that what I'm claiming in this book is attainable. It's also why we spent seven chapters and a mountain of responsibilities and warnings to get here. Today, it's not hard to transmit; it just takes arduous personal transformation to do so effectively. Now that I've hopefully inspired you, let's come back down and discuss the groups you'll encounter along the journey.

I've narrowed down six different types of people who will hear and receive, hear and apply, hear and champion, hear and discard, hear and attack, or hear and forget your world-shaping ideas. They are as follows: ***Naysayers, Skeptics, Neutrals, Accepters, Adopters, and Apostles.***

Let's start in the negative category and move forward. I always like a big crescendo, so we'll lead up to it.

NAYSAYERS

The first and largest group of people you'll run into as you present your world-shaping ideas are the Naysayers. These might also be called "haters" or, at worst, "trolls." Naysayers will *never* support your idea, no matter what it's. They won't even read or listen to you if it doesn't line up with their personal, and often narrow, worldview. (Remember, your ideas need to be presented as inclusively as possible, but it still won't matter much to a Naysayer).

These are the types who call anyone not precisely lined up with their religious beliefs, "heretics." Or those who refused to subscribe to any religion at all would call anything presented religiously as "Jesus Freaked." This is the Trump supporter who won't consider anything outside of Trump's tweets. Or the liberal who still thinks Hillary should be the only president and continues to broadcast it to anyone willing to listen.

They're the people at the opposite ends of the 50/50 polarizing bands. They won't get you, because you aren't *exactly* like them. They'll question your education, your social status, your mental state. They will attempt to tear you down in every way possible. Don't worry; five minutes before, they were trashing Taylor Swift or shouting down Anderson Cooper on CNN or Michael Watters on Fox News. It's just what they do.

How to interact with the Naysayer
You don't.

Responding to the Naysayer should be avoided at all costs, for two reasons. First, they will likely never be swayed. You'll spend way too much time and effort trying to convince them otherwise. Second, and more important, the reason you need to convince them is often rooted in Ego. Sorry, but it's a trap to test your belief in your worth (Chapter 2). You've already recalibrated (Chapter 3). Don't go back down this road.

SKEPTICS

Skeptics are different. While naysayers will disagree with you because you aren't precisely like them, skeptics will disagree with you because they *don't believe* what you're saying yet. They're far more educated and nuanced than most naysayers. *They can back up why* they don't believe you.

That's fine if not essential.

They're looking at your world-shaping idea from inside their own worldview. Remember the story of the three blind men touching different parts of an elephant and all three coming up with three completely different conclusions as to what they were touching? The Skeptic is touching one area of the elephant, where to him or her you are speaking from a different place on the pachyderm.

How to interact with Skeptics

Engage them! (oh, please engage them)

More than any other group (other than Apostles), these are the most important people to help refine and affirm your world-shaping idea. Going back to the elephant, instead of arguing from your side of the animal or trying to convince them what they're feeling is wrong, take off the blindfolds! There are a few ways to do this.

First, remember that you need to understand all aspects of your idea, and you need an immense amount of grounding *outside* your belief system. If you can argue your point using science and data, it's hard for the skeptic to deny what you're saying. Again, they may not like your thoughts, and especially your conclusions, but they can't well argue the facts. Don't get frustrated with them; in many cases, they may be wiser than you are.

Second, ask skeptics all about them – their beliefs, their hopes and dreams. Get them to engage you both inside and outside your big idea. Take the time to dialog and listen to their backstory. That will help you understand where they are coming from and how their past has influenced their worldview. Skeptics can quickly become naysayers if you fail to handle them with dignity.

Because skeptics are often more educated, they can jump from skeptics to Apostles if you present your world-shaping idea with empathy and grace. It may take considerable time and attention, but when the light dawns in the heart of a skeptic it shines the brightest.

A single skeptic comes to your idea with a cadre of others behind him or her who subscribe to similar beliefs. Win him or her over to your world-shaping idea and he or she may broadcast your idea to a portion of humanity you would never reach on your own.

NEUTRALS

Chances are you've been a Neutral. People have recommended a book to you that you never read. Shared ideas that never took. Passionately asked you to change a certain trait that you may have brushed off. I was a neutral for many years of my life. I didn't feel like I needed to learn anything. I had a handle on life.

I designed the first four chapters of this book to shift many of us out of neutral, and I'll bet that if you're reading this book in chunks you recognize that you're becoming less and less of a Neutral.

Neutrals are most steeped in Ego. They are the type who won't follow a person's Instagram page… unless that person is famous, or unless someone liked his or her post first. They don't think they need much in life, unless that person is ahead of them economically, socially, and the like. They will most likely come around to your side if you become famous enough, but remember, that may or may not happen for you, nor is it your goal.

How to interact with a Neutral:
Cautiously.

This group can beat you down, because they'll zap your energy and momentum. They don't mean to, but they just can't receive what you have to say. You'll find yourself either spending all your time trying to convince them, or you'll get too frustrated that they aren't listening. Realize that they can't. To them, you don't have the weight behind you to allow them to consider your ideas.

Always thank them for comments, if they leave them, but don't push them further like you would with a skeptic. If they are friends, don't disown them; realize that you have probably been a neutral at some point in their lives.

Okay, now we're getting to the good parts.

ACCCEPTERS

Accepters are those who *will* read your blog, watch your video, and subscribe to your channel. They're generally more positive and more empathetic people. They're considerate of new ideas. They'll leave comments like "Awesome post!" or "Great Word!" (there's often an exclamation point or emoji attached). They may even share your posts on their pages, leading to a large group of new followers. Accepters are usually more centrist and can see more than one side to an opinion or idea.

They may ask questions like the skeptic, but usually from a more optimistic perspective. You're more likely to have friends who are accepters because they value you, but beware, accepter friends are often less loyal than accepters you've never met. Friends are often accepting until there's a cost involved, like paying for your book or taking twenty minutes out of their busy day to watch your YouTube video. Non-friend Accepters have found you through their own searches and needs, and they're more likely to fulfill any requests you may present them.

How to interact with an Accepter:

Thank them, encourage them, challenge them, but don't feed ego because of them.

This is a great group to have, because they help build credibility, but they're accepting of your ideas like they are accepting of a myriad of other voices and faces they interact with, like, and subscribe to. They're by nature, more able to hear your ideas. They'll be your biggest positive group at first, but because there isn't too much cost involved they are likely less attached to your idea than you think. This isn't meant to be discouraging, but if you get too focused on the number of Accepters you generate, you'll start feeding Ego again.

Remember, a person who receives a million "likes" on a Facebook or Instagram post probably has 950,000 (or more) accepters attached to that post. Those

Accepters will leave your page or channel and like five or six other posts by different leaders, celebrities, and other friends that very day.

Still, engage and interact with this group. Accepters can become Adopters quickly if they feel valued. Remember, they come from a more optimistic place, so challenge and encourage them to better subscribe to and apply your world-shaping idea in their own lives. The longer you engage with an Accepter the better, if you feel he or she start moving closer to what you are presenting. Don't pressure him or her too far, though; it's easy to come off needy or pushy. He or she won't become a Naysayer, but likely unfriend you or unsubscribe to your channel without you ever being aware.

ADOPTERS

Unlike an Accepter who *listens* to your ideas, Adopters will take your ideas and *apply them* to their lives. Adopters won't just comment on your post; they'll share stories of how your thoughts and words impacted them personally. When they share on social media they usually tie their post share into a personal example.

There's far more weight coming from Adopters, because the idea reached them at their core, and it shows in how they present. They are more than positive; they are motivated. With every comment from an Adopter on your social media or blog, her or she has probably shared the idea with eight to sixteen of his or her friends. The circle widens quickly with Adopters, because they're impacting others who are likely to impact more, and so on and so forth.

Think about the moments you've been an Adopter. It may have come from a thought in a book or a Ted talk, but it could have just as easily come from a movie or song. You've heard something powerful enough to make a difference in your life, and you've broadcasted it to others.

This is really the group for which you've developed your world-shaping idea. You aren't going through this process, painstakingly journeying down this path, just to be heard. *You're aiming to be applied.*

How to interact with an Adopter:
Inspire, engage, and challenge them. Create channels for other adopters to connect with each other.

Ask them to broadcast your ideas to those with greater influence.

Adopters are your ambassadors. They may communicate your ideas even better than you can, because your ideas have worked positively in their own lives. You need to get involved in their lives so they feel a part of who you are and what you're doing. If you receive an email, engage. If you get a social media post, repost or Private Message them directly.

Build a community for these people to engage and interact through. Facebook has great options for this. Create a private or public group and encourage adopters to participate. Offer incentives and weekly testimonials. Ask Adopters to promote you to those with real influence in media, publishing, and communications.

As much as I don't like the term, Adopters will become part of your "tribe." The difference is that your tribe isn't based on a worldview, political bias, or personal or religious preference, it's built around an idea. Your "tribe" should look as disparate as America; it should be a "rainbow coalition" of inclusion where many who may never see eye to eye share similar positive and impactful stories gleaned from your world-shaping idea.

APOSTLES

Apostles are a rarity. More than just individuals who hear and apply your words, Apostles want to connect to you personally. They believe in your words so strongly that they're willing to do whatever it takes to see them furthered in society.

They'll write personal emails to you, sharing how your words have impacted them, and, more important, how they want to be part of your movement. They will connect to you at a deeper level than the Adopter, and they can become a little too fervent if not careful. Remember, your world-shaping idea is never about you. Don't let an Apostle shift the focus from the idea to the person presenting it.

Still, they'll broadcast your ideas to anyone willing to listen. They'll help facilitate meetings with highly influential people. They'll set up their own blogs to talk about your ideas. They'll weekly, or even daily, post quotes from your work.

How to interact with an Apostle

Mentor them.

Apostles are your legacy builders. They'll carry your ideas forward and proclaim your ideas in their own language (we'll discuss that in future chapters). They need to know everything about your world-shaping idea. Where Adopters receive the key nuggets of thought, present your apostles with *the stories behind your ideas*. Where did your ideas come from? What have you learned along the way? What dangers did you come against in the discovery of your idea?

Think of an Apostle like an apprentice. Pour everything into them in hopes they'll carry a new mantle forward in the future. It's a mantle shaped by you, but one that carries their own learning and insights.

Don't think Apostles will just fall out of the trees. Out of ten thousand Accepters, you may generate one hundred Adopters and only one Apostle. Be grateful for every Apostle you receive. It means your idea is truly world-shaping.

Hopefully, your Apostles will not all have the worldview, religious, or ideological proclivity as you, but they might, depending on your idea. Regardless, encourage them to be nuanced and inclusive when sharing your insights.

Apostles easily integrate into your social Twelve, as discussed in the last chapter. They probably rarely will break into the Three, and that's okay. Don't share all your deepest secrets with Apostles. Keep the conversations focused on your world-shaping ideas, but allow them to peer into your life at a deeper level.

Practically, you can set up private Facebook groups or instigate SKYPE video conferences with your Apostles. Connect them with each other *after* you've mentored them for a while. Their collective insights will radically further your ideas.

IN CONCLUSION

I hope that breaking down these individuals help encourage you to move forward. Don't get beaten down by the Naysayers. You'll probably have more of them at first, but keep pressing forward. Remember, your accepter group will grow as your influence and status grows, so don't get too heady as those numbers increase. You're looking for Skeptics, Adopters, and

Apostles. That should be your aim. Read every comment, post, and email you receive and see if they fit into one of those three categories. Hopefully these three groups will be a collection of radically different people, all with different beliefs, social status, ethnicities, and income levels.

If you can build a coalition like that, you're on your way to becoming an MLK2.0. As your influence grows, the circle will widen. Remain focused on where your worth comes from, don't let Ego have any say in the matter, and above all, never stop educating yourself forward.

Now that you know who you're going to meet along with your world-shaping idea, it's time to figure out which medium or mediums you'll use to transmit.

MLK2.0

CHAPTER 9
PRESENTATION

(What is your method and medium of transmission)

"If I cannot do great things, I can do small things in a great way."
Martin Luther King Jr.

You should now have a clear idea of who will receive your world-shaping idea. Next, you must determine the method or methods of transmission of broadcast. There are numerous transmission avenues now available, which we'll discuss in a few moments. But before you determine what medium you're going to use to transmit, you need to determine *how* you'll present your world-shaping idea. Many people can't just hear an idea; it needs to be communicated in a way that's palatable and reproducible. Below are four ways to share your world-shaping idea.

CRAFT METAPHORS

Any writer worth his or her salt recognizes the great power found in the wielding of the metaphor. Aristotle, one of the most influential and brightest philosophical and creative minds in history, described the effective use of metaphor as, "a sign of genius." Below I'll answer why and uncover why it's so powerful for your world-shaping idea.

Great metaphors transcend a person's worldview preconceptions.

We live in a post-modern society. Each of us has a belief system by which we live, more or less, but as participants in this post-modern world, we may hold strongly to our beliefs, but so do the rest of the participants in society. In America, beliefs, or worldviews, collide every nanosecond. We're a nation of immigrants, each with a broad range of worldviews.

We must acknowledge and respect the views of others or face judgment and vilification from our more tolerant brothers and sisters. This leads to avoidance of certain topics, because our opinions of those topics are deeply entrenched in our worldviews. I'm reminded of a country music song, where a heartbroken man tells a friend that he can talk together about anything but "politics, religion, and *her*."

A great metaphor transcends all of that. When Jesus Christ stated, "The Kingdom of Heaven is like *a seed*," those listening didn't question: "Is it an existentialist seed? Is it a nihilistic seed? Is it a deistic seed?"

No, it was simply a seed! By using the daily and the recognizable to define and redefine an aspect of your product or service, you create bridges beyond stalwart beliefs and preconceptions that often breed animosity, disdain, and distrust.

Great metaphors allow the listener to delve deeper into the metaphor itself.

A great metaphor allows the listener to meditate on the idea and search it out in deeper ways. The listener extracts new and relevant information beyond the spoken words. When Jesus said the Kingdom of

Heaven was like a seed, the metaphor didn't end. Want to learn more about the Kingdom of Heaven? Sit with a farmer. I believe the depth of the metaphor is limitless. A friend of mine once described Jesus' metaphoric power as operating from, "profound simplicity." This should be your aim. Drill down to the most simplistic concept, but one rich with future possibilities.

Great metaphors can create new relevancy to concepts and ideas that appear stagnant or single-sided.

In 2013, I wrote a book entitled, *Parables and Parallels: Modern Day Insights into Many Ancient Words*. Featuring 26 chapters of insights on Biblical scripture, the book often uses modern day metaphors such as the DVD Director's Commentary, the storyline of the hit action series, *24,* and "body snatching" alien films. In utilizing these metaphors, I extracted profound and relevant ideas and concepts that, inside their own theological confines, appeared stagnant, hyper-moral, and restrictive.

By utilizing the metaphor, you not only transcend a person's worldview, but you can also alter and even shatter their preconceptions of a concept, idea, or belief.

Metaphor is more than just a simile; it's *the story you tell* behind your idea. You can craft that story in a paragraph, or you can turn it into a children's book, a short film, a novel, or a screenplay. I have a few world-shaping ideas that have become children's books and short screenplays. We remember ideas better when they're presented in story form.

Regardless of how you chose to use your metaphors… make sure you use them often in defining and describing your world-shaping ideas. Run your metaphors by your Three and Twelve and see if they can grasp your concepts instantly. If not, dig deeper.

ASK QUESTIONS:

We've talked about this in past chapters, but inductive (self discovery) over deductive (instruction) approaches work best when broadcasting something never spoken nor considered before. You want the audience to learn alongside of you. Don't speak at, or worse, speak down to you audience. Present your ideas in the form of questions, and allow listeners to draw their own insights and conclusions and feel part of the process. They are much more likely to share if they believe the idea has, in part, come through their own discovery.

Take questions that you birthed in your social media posts and explore them in more detail on blog posts and Video Blogs. Start the conversation (and even blog title) with a question, then answer it in a way that keeps the conversation open for the listener or reader. Hebraic thought centers around the idea that the wise don't learn answers, but continue to ask better questions. I love that mantra. Continuing to ask questions will further develop your world-shaping idea, even after you feel it's ready for transmission.

CONSIDER INTERVIEWS

Once a world-shaping idea takes root in your life, it coats your life and influences your actions. There's no better way of getting other people to consider that idea more fully than by using it in interviews with influential people.

People, especially great thinkers, love to be interviewed. You can usually set up meetings with influential people if you're inspiring enough that they see the value in an interview.

Once you set up the interview, craft questions around your world-shaping idea. Don't bait and switch and/or attack someone with your idea. Present it in a manner that's winsome and inclusive.

If you do it right, you may likely transplant your interviewee into an adopter, as most leaders/thinkers recognize the value in new, revolutionary ideas. Plus, you'll draw in the listeners/fans of the person you're interviewing. This can build your influential base quickly.

POST INSIGHTS ON OTHERS' SOCIAL MEDIA PAGES

Another way to generate influence is to post your one to two sentence thoughts in the comments of others' social media pages. This is especially powerful on Instagram, because it houses the broadest range of individuals. Most comments on social media come from Accepters, so saying something fresh and relevant draws interest from both the one who originally posted and those who see your post comment. Add to the conversation (act like an Accepter), then insert your world-shaping thoughts at the end of the comment (finish as an Adopter).

Do this well and you can generate a far larger friendship base (or tribe) than just posting on your own. Plus, you never know which of your new followers may be a close friend of the original poster and can recommend for that influential person to consider your idea, and take a look at your blog, YouTube page, or social media platforms.

Now that you have an idea of how to present your idea, the rest of the chapter is devoted to uncovering the variety of broadcasting mediums available to you. I've also included the approximate costs and learning curve to help you make your decisions.

BLOG:

Cost: Minimal
Learning Curve: Nominal

A blog is the easiest and least time intrusive way to begin broadcasting your world-shaping idea. Blog sites pretty much do the work for you, allowing you to focus on your content and presentation and not get encumbered with tricky things like coding and SEO strategies.

Blogs also allow you to share small digestible snipets of information, over the creation of say an ebook, which will take longer to set up and produce. In addition, most blog readers are more willing to accept less grammatically adept writings than they would if you were to present them with a published book. If you're not yet an expert in creative writing and grammar, a blog is a great introduction into that world. You can use your blog as the impetus for your mini e-book or final published book. Plus, you can collect critical data and insights from your readers along the way. Your world-shaping idea doesn't have to result in a published book. A blog may be just as effective at communicating powerful insights that take root quickly.

Practically, there have been a number of free blog services available in the past like Wordpress and Blogspot. Personally I would check out WIX.com and SquareSpace.com. These relatively new online platforms offer far more template flexibility and style, and the learning curve is minimal (about 3 hours on WIX and around 45 minutes on SquareSpace) if you have any basic computer knowledge. SquareSpace also offers an incredible range of flexibility and style enhancements, if you know CSS. Take heart, what you don't know you can find and apply with a quick five minute Google Search.

Although setting up these sites is free, you'll pay for your personal domain name as well as a hosting fee that will run under $200 or so per year.

Think about your blog like a retail product and try to brand it as visually pleasing as possible. Consider the name, work on a logo, choose your template wisely. Make sure that you have plenty of calls-to-action on each page and post, like an email signup form, online polls, or special giveaways.

YOUTUBE (OR THE LIKE) VIDEO CHANNEL

Cost: $300 - $700 in equipment

Learning Curve: Moderate, but be prepared for lots of editing hours per video

Due to the increased technological advances in online video, text based blogging has been overshadowed by Video Blogging. Sites like YouTube, Metacafe, and VIMEO offer free or nearly free video uploading opportunities, but I would start with (and probably stick with) YouTube. YouTube constantly innovates and, like Google over Bing, internet users congregate on YouTube far more than any other video site.

Video Blogging equipment isn't cheap and the learning curve is steep, but if you have a dynamic presence, know the formatting, and/or have the time to learn, YouTube offers a far broader audience than blogging ever could. Make sure you invest in quality equipment or you'll be judged and discarded quickly. It would be tragic to sacrifice a world-shaping idea for the sake of saving a few hundred bucks.

Your video blog will probably be more talking than showing (we'll talk about making movies shortly), so make sure you incorporate dynamic graphic slides and other graphics into your video presentations. Be sure to keep your videos fairly short. YouTube delineates between videos that are under and over twenty minutes. Make sure to optimize your keywords. Try to choose interesting and broad reaching keywords to attract a greater audience.

Be engaging, but confident, in your videos.

It also helps to have a blog for the viewer to visit after he or she has heard your idea.

SNAPCHATS AND INSTAGRAM STORIES

Cost: Usually just the cost of the iphone or android device
Learning Curve: Nominal

Millennials (if that's your audience) like things in bite size, digestible, and often discarded formats. SnapChats and Instagram Stories allow you to share quick ideas without having to invest in the broadcast quality gear necessary for most YouTube video presentations. Just turn your mobile phone around and record yourself or have someone record for you.

Both platforms allow for simple text and graphics, which adds dynamism over just a talking head, but the medium itself prohibits you from getting very deep with your presentations. Most SnapChats and Instagram Stories are quick and pithy, if not downright pointless (here's me eating Sushi in Chicago, here's me falling while skateboarding, etc.), so you're competing with some pretty random content. Getting too heady or complex may lose the audience.

Still, along with your social media, these mediums allow your subscribers to view you more intimately and connect with you on a deeper level. I wouldn't recommend it as your sole source of transmission, but as a powerful additional tool.

PODCASTS

Cost: About $300 in equipment (and you'll need editing software like Garage Band)

Learning Curve: Moderate, but less than YouTube videos

If you're too shy for video or just don't want to face that level of a learning curve, Podcasts are a fantastic alternative. You can set up a podcast on the Apple Store, Bluberry, SoundCloud, or others at little or no cost. You'll, however, have to pay for broadcasting equipment, such as a microphone and headset to create a professionally sounding presentation.

Podcasts are powerful in a few ways. First, instead of just reading your thoughts, listeners can hear the passion behind your ideas. Your personality will shine through on a podcast, and that can be powerful and winsome. Second, podcast platforms are keyword searchable. You can easily be found by a large audience if you optimize your keywords. Third, interviewing others is both easy and the accepted norm on podcasts.

To interview on YouTube, you must travel to the individual's home or have him or her in your home or studio. With podcasting, you can interview remotely and retain relatively clean broadcast quality.

Make sure you brand your podcast well, with a dynamic name and a powerful logo and icon. You want to stand out among the panoply of other podcast offerings. Thankfully, there are hundreds of sites and blogs that offer help on how to set up, run, and market your podcast. What you don't know now about podcasting today, you'll easily learn by tomorrow.

MOVIES AND SHORT FILMS

Cost: Thousands to Millions of Dollars
Learning Curve: Heavy and excellence is key, as you're competing with the best of the best

Movies like *The Matrix* presented powerful ideas (unintended or not) that led to millions of hours in thought and dialog since their releases. By presenting your world-shaping idea around a well written, filmed, and produced film or short film, you can tap into a far broader audience and incite greater universal dialog than you could just presenting facts and figures.

Stories are long form metaphors. Many stories are a series of metaphors, but stories, if done well, are enjoyable forms of entertainment, and your ideas can collide into the viewer's psyche without effort.

Still, creating a film is hard work and there are a lot of costs involved. If you have the time, talent, or are already in the field or have a personal friend or relative in the industry, making a film around your world-shaping idea can be the most powerful tool in your arsenal. Here are a few considerations.

1. **Hire a professional screenwriter.** Even if you have your film idea laid out well, hire a screenwriter to finalize it. There are numerous books on screenplay writing, but it pays to go to the experts. Without the right format and intrigue from your story, all the acting, lighting, and film effects fall flat. You can also present your final screenplay on various critique sites for further review or submit it into a local or national film festival.

2. **Hire great actors**. Don't just throw friends into your film or short film. Produce it with excellence, even it's just going up on YouTube or Vimeo. The better the quality, the more likely

it can not only go viral, but remain top of mind. Pick your actors well and you may produce something that lasts for decades.

3. **Hire a great crew, especially the lighting crew.** There's nothing worse than a poorly lit film. It destroys the message and the acting, because your focus remains fixed on the poor lighting quality. Make sure your film looks professional and dynamic.

There are ways to do all of these things on the cheap and there are numerous techniques of filming, so study your craft and pick a film style that works for your idea and budget.

E BOOKS OR PUBLISHED BOOKS

Cost: Under $1,000, if you self-publish and hire an establish cover designer

Learning Curve: Fairly light in technical requirements, but more intensive to learn great book writing skills

Robert McKee, the world-renowned scriptwriter, starts his seminal book on scriptwriting for film and television with the following assertion: if you want to make a movie–*write a book*. The reason is simple, only a small portion of screenplays ever get made into films or television pilots, whereas books are ubiquitous and relatively inexpensive to develop and publish.

Books over blogs give the reader something to tactically share with friends and relatives; it carries greater weight. It also allows the reader to engage at a different level. Remember, books happen *with you*. Books are more likely to help shape someone's worldview quicker with a book than a film.

With a screenplay, you're also fixed to within 105 and 120 pages. With books, you can write a short 20 E Book or a 500 page well researched tome. The choice is up to you. My personal works have ranged anywhere between 25 pages and 300 pages, depending on the idea and its complexity.

Practically, most of the technical requirements for writing a book can be found, and templates downloaded, with a quick search on the internet. You'll need to use a program like Microsoft Word or Adobe InDesign to layout your pages, so there's a little cost involved if you don't have these programs. *I would also recommend hiring a professional to design your book cover*. A poor cover often equates to a discarded book.

Print on demand services like CreateSpace and Ingram's Lightning Source provide nearly one stop offerings for book publishing, printing, distribution, and marketing. Other sites, like Goodreads.com and NoiseTrade.com, allow you to interact with other authors and thinkers, share your compelling story, and sell and/or promote your book. With every download of your book on NoiseTrade, you receive the email address of the downloader, so you can build a database of followers relatively easily. They can also leave a donation with the download, allowing you to make a little revenue on a supposedly free book giveaway. Noisetrade, and sites like it, are a great way to pre-market your final book, collect feedback, and generate a decent database of engaged followers.

YOUR MEDIUM? YOU CHOOSE!

Chances are after reading this list of mediums, you'll resonate with the avenue that's right for you. You'll probably use more than one of these transmission mediums in the original telling of your world-shaping idea. You should also move from simpler formats to more complex and costly avenues as your idea gains traction. Make sure you start with one of these mediums, and ensure that you stay up to date on your social media platforms to support it.

Next, I'll show you how to gain further traction as your idea makes a greater impact on the world.

MLK2.0

CHAPTER 10
FOLLOW-THROUGH
(Creating "stickability" with your world-shaping idea)

Awareness of your world-shaping idea is one thing. Follow-through is just as, if not more, important. You want to make sure that your idea sticks in the minds of your listeners and society. You must spend as much time cultivating your world-shaping idea as you did discovering it. This chapter will help you develop techniques and applications for the greatest amount of follow-through and continued exposure. I recommend that you practice all of the techniques and ideas presented in this chapter.

ELEVATE YOUR MEDIUMS

Once you've had success in one or a few of the methods of transmission (for example, blogging and podcasting), consider elevating to more extensive and expensive mediums like book writing, documentaries, or full-length films. Hopefully, as your audience grows, so has the breadth of their experience and status. This will make it easier to find others to help you in your future ventures.

Cultivate relationships with influential and accomplished people, but be honest and upfront about your desire to recruit them for their abilities. Don't promote one individual over another based on his or her status or success, but recognize that certain people can help take your idea to levels you may not be able to achieve on your own.

SPEAK IN PUBLIC

Another way to test your ideas in the general populace is through public speaking. There are numerous opportunities available to those willing to make the effort and get out there and market themselves. Consider starting with your local chamber of commerce or rotary club; they're often looking for guest speakers. So, too, are business networking groups like Mastermind or LeTip International, Inc. If your idea pertains to children or teens, consider speaking at school assemblies or perhaps at your local church youth group.

As you develop your oratory skills, you may speak at conferences and symposiums and other informational-based events. Make sure you set up your website or blog to include marketing your speaking abilities as well as spotlighting a few speaking topics.

Speaking events allow you to craft and hone a concept for a book or short e-book. My last book, *CRE8TVE SUCCESS*, was birthed through an hour long talk I gave at a local Mastermind Lunch gathering in Nashville. Always record your talks so you can go over them at a later date and extract information for further use, especially if there's a Q&A session after or during your talk.

Personally, I transcribe, then record my talks prior to the actual speaking date. This way I can both memorize my talk, as well as break it down into segments that work later as chapters or section breaks. My talks often become the impetus for detailed written outlines.

Use metaphors often in your public speaking opportunities. Remember, unlike a book, which moves at the reader's pace, the audience is processing your talk at a much more rapid speed. If your world-shaping idea is complex, it may not register quickly. By breaking down your idea metaphorically and telling stories or anecdotes that relate to your world-shaping idea, your audience will remember the story over the idea itself. You can always encourage your audience to go deeper with you through one-on-one consultations, Skype calls, or private Facebook groups.

SEEK OUT GOOD P.R.

As you develop and grow, I recommend hiring a PR team to support your promotional efforts. It's possible to get local coverage on television or on news sites using your own press releases and personal hustle. To really accelerate your message nationally it's best to have a strong PR team working with you.

FOLLOW-THROUGH: CREATING STICKABILITY...

Still, be cautious. Remember, this is your world-shaping idea. Don't let them distort it into something it's not. Work with your PR team to craft an effective message, then let them do the legwork necessary to get your name and idea out into the broader world.

There are numerous types of PR agencies. Some agencies require money up front, but guarantee a fix number of viewers or readers based on their relationships with media outlets. Others will take a sizable fee with each speaking, writing, or guest blogging opportunity they acquire.

I have a strong relationship with Marsha Friedman, author of *Celebritize Yourself*. Marsha offers a pay-upfront PR service that guarantees a high *minimum* number of viewers, readers, and opportunities with the top media outlets. Her forty year history has placed her in front of some of the biggest names in broadcast, digital, and print media, and her rolodex is filled with the names you, and your world-shaping idea, will want to be associated with. You can learn more about Marsha and her team at *www.emsincorporated.com*.

GUEST BLOG/GUEST PODCAST

When you first shared your world-shaping idea, you sought out influential leaders to interview on your podcast. As your idea gains traction, it's highly probable that others will ask you to contribute to their blogs and podcasts.

Always research those offering you this opportunity. You want to come off knowledgeable and engaging when you speak with them on their podcasts. You also want to make sure your guest blog ties into that blogger's overall story. Don't attempt to steal their listeners or fans, but use this as an opportunity to reach an audience you might not have discovered on your own.

Many of the larger blogs offer great writers the opportunity to write for their sites (ChristianPost.com, Patheos, Edge.org, etc.), often for free, especially if your idea is centered around a certain ideology or belief, but most ideological or religious (or anti-religious) blogs, have a focused agenda and narrow viewpoint. Don't get categorized in an arena you don't want to be too associated with.

YOUR GOAL: ADOPTION INTO THEIR OWN LANGUAGE

As your world-shaping idea continues to grow into a prosperous tree of insight and wisdom, don't be surprised if others begin to graft into your tree with their own offshoots. A person rooted in Ego will fight this. You must not.

You want your world-shaping idea to take on a life of its own. One of the ways to make this happen is to always ask questions of your audience. Get them to explain how adopting your idea has transformed their lives. As they take greater ownership of your idea, they will start to recast it in their own language. Remember to mentor your apostles and continue to engage your skeptics, and adopters.

YOUR VISION: FIELD TRANFORMING LEADERSHIP

The goal of your idea is not just to educate or even inspire; it's to transform.

One of my favorite books in the last ten years is a rather unknown book entitled, *Existentialism and the*

Modern Predicament by F.H. Heinemann. In the book, Heinemann references five types of spiritual leaders. For the sake of brevity, I will focus on two. *The field dependent leader* and *the field influencing leader*.

The field dependent leader is the type of leader who can only influence his or her followers in one area of their lives. He's truly the big fish in a vsmall pond. He's the president in his own Matrix. To expand his leadership role, he must create subcultures into other domains so that he can lead across multiple disciplines and influential bases.

For example, let's take Christian leadership. It primarily works (out of its own making) as a personal choice and a personal relationship. Through Darwinian science and Separation of Church and State and its own hypocrisy, Christianity appears to get pushed further out of the mainstream culture. To gain more leadership, it must create new classes in other domains, like Christian films, Christian books, Christian music, Christian education, etc. Too bad if the people who engage in these subset arenas often detach further from the mainstream; it allows the field dependent leader more leadership ability and, in some cases, greater financial opportunities.

T*he field influencing leader* doesn't need that. Instead, whatever idea the leader brings to the society has the ability to "influence" other domains. Instead of creating subclasses, other domains base their insights and actions around the ideas of the field influencing leader. Their ideas help redefine medicine, science, education, commerce, and the like. A field influencing leader influences from the outside in.

Metaphorically, a field dependent leader forces his or her followers to put their eggs into his or her single basket and keep them there as long as possible, and a field influencing leader creates multiple baskets, where each egg is placed into its own new basket.

This is as far as Heinemann goes. As profound as the field influencing leader is, and as shallow as the field dependent leader can become, there's a sixth way that Heinemann failed to discover.

The Field Transforming Leader.

The field transforming leader also comes affixed with an idea or many ideas. Instead of speaking to his or her tribe and creating subcultures like the field dependent leader or just influencing other spheres like the field influencing leader, his or her ideas *transform* every arena and domain it comes into contact with. It doesn't matter the ideology that birthed the idea; its power transcends ideology and makes a positive difference, regardless of the beliefs and preconceptions of its adopters. It's a universal and holistic transformation.

Metaphorically, the transforming leader still offers one basket, but when any egg is dropped into the basket, it emerges with more positive power and insight than it had prior to having been dropped in the basket.

Your world-shaping idea should be field transforming. Whatever you claim and hypothesize should be able to be dropped into any domain and make a more powerful and positive difference in that field than had been previously discovered by its current experts and ambassadors.

One of the reasons your world-shaping idea can accomplish this is that it's tied to objective realities like understandings of the brain, the body, or statistical data. It's also focused on objective outcomes, not subjective actions. You're not attempting to validate a worldview, belief nor political opinion, you're grounding your ideas in facticity *for the benefit of humanity*.

Your world-shaping idea may be theoretical at first, but as it gains traction, others will attempt to validate it in their own domains. In other words, if your world-shaping idea is potent and valid enough, others will continue to do the work for you. Celebrate this. Encourage this. Let wiser men and women uncover new revelations in their own domains through applying your world-shaping idea.

Congratulations, you've generated and cultivated a world-shaping idea into the world. I believe the world will be better for it. Now it's time to help generate that difference throughout the course of history. You're ready to build your personal legacy.

MLK2.0

CHAPTER 11
LEGACY
(Shaping this, and future, generations)

As amazing as Martin Luther King Jr. was and as transformative as his words and speeches have been throughout history, there's an asterisk attached to his name. MLK was also known for his extramarital affairs as noted in the newly released FBI files.

Many can discount or turn a blind eye to these revelations based on the impact he made in history, but sadly that asterisk will always hang over his name. MLK built a legacy, but it came affixed with conditions. This book was written to help you discover your world-shaping idea and build a legacy without an asterisk.

This book wasn't meant to be read in a single sitting. To believe you now "have it" after reading this book and can quickly move forward on your world-shaping idea is, most likely, a fallacy.

The first four chapters take time to develop in your life. It may take months and even years to cultivate the fertile character and humble soil necessary to sustain a world-shaping idea. For me, it took even longer. I'm still not there, which is why I'm writing this book instead of being heralded on television and in the news media repeatedly. I've come to realize that it may not be my calling to be in the global spotlight, but I do know how to foster and encourage the next great world-shaper. I do know what it will take to become an MLK2.0.

Your world-shaping status and ability doesn't need to be affixed with an asterisk. You can transcend. You

LEGACY: SHAPING GENERATIONS

can elevate the game. In Chapter Three, I showed you why you must. You should now have a cadre of supporters looking up to you. It's not about you anymore. To build a historical legacy the right way, you must keep all of this in mind.

Muhammed Ali had a man on his payroll whose responsibility was little more than to "hype" him up. He made his living constantly showering Ali with praise and adornment. Don't do this. Instead, you should have those around you who are constantly admonishing you to stay humble, to not let success and all that goes with it get into your head. Remember, without humility, new world-shaping ideas will get quickly pushed out. There's only so much room in your head, and world-shaping ideas are most often spoken in a quieter tone than Ego's louder words of distorted praise.

I hope I can be one of these people in your life who, after reading this book, keeps you grounded. I hope I had a part of building your legacy without an asterisk attached. Below are five final ways that can help you in the process.

1. KEEP YOUR CHARACTER

We all have a past. Many of us probably wish to see some of it erased. The idea that it can come back to haunt us can grow more prevalent as you gain further exposure. Regardless of where you've been or what you've done, use this immediate moment as your opportunity to build powerful and positive character moving forward.

You're not a rock star. You're not a celebrity. Your success and status grew *out of an idea*. It's an idea in which, if you're honest, you can't take much credit. It came through Inspiration, through listening to and applying the words of others far wiser than you, and through the shaping of those in your inner circles and close relations. Reflect on that when the media comes running and your subscribers reach into the hundreds of thousands or more.

Many, especially the young, tend to spin out of control after becoming better known. There's a sense of invincibility that Ego attempts to bring onto the successful and famous. It's a trap and an illusion. Remember, if Ego can discount you, it can erode your world-shaping idea in the process.

Stay strong in character, love everyone, remain humble.

Every famous person was just an average citizen at some point in their history. This should bring encouragement and opportunity to the citizen and responsibility to the famous. It should certainly place responsibility on you.

Don't think this means that just your ideology or faith can sustain your character either. Some of the greatest leaders in Religious thought imploded through poor character choices or unchecked Ego. Don't let your name and your world-shaping idea become affixed with an asterisk to excuse your poor character.

I encourage you to wake up each morning before the opportunities and accolades of the day overtake you, stare into the mirror, and say, "I *will* keep my character today." If you become a world-shaper, if you've been blessed with a world-shaping idea, you now have an accountability to the world. An accountability to history. It's not worth losing it over a few moments of unchecked rush, a sense of grandiosity, or a poorly based decision you'll regret moments later.

2. SPOTLIGHT OTHERS

One of the ways to build a legacy is to take the focus off yourself and encourage and support those journeying alongside of you. *You'll* only take your world-shaping idea so far. To build a legacy requires others to carry the mantle forward.

The original idea may have come from you, but through cultivation it has no doubt taken on a life of its own. As others contribute to the idea, don't forget to credit them in the process.

In the book *Good to Great*, Jim Collins describes the *window/mirror* leadership concept. It means that when times are good, a true leader always looks through the window to see and credit those who supported him or her. When times are difficult, a leader looks into the mirror and reflects on where and how he or she could have addressed things better.

It's not always easy to do, especially if someone else gets more credit for your ideas or your mentoring.

Years ago I mentored a young man, pouring my life into him for about two years. One day he came to me excited about a new position he had just been given. I had wanted that position and the status that came with it. After he left, I thought *I trained this young man, everything that got him the position came from my thoughts and expertise.* The wallowing lasted a few hours, until I realized that was the greatest compliment I could have received.

That man was elevated because I had poured into his life. He had applied my ideas and considerations, and the result was new opportunity and greater recognition. The position didn't come to me, but it didn't matter. It came *from me*. I went back to that young man and apologized for an attitude he didn't know I had taken. Two weeks later I was given an even greater opportunity.

Don't worry about credit. Focus on *transformation*. There's too much credit being sought today, especially at the highest levels of government. Be more of a man or woman than that. Change the world. Change history. Let that be enough for you, then highlight everyone who helped you make it happen and consider all those whose lives have been altered because of your world-shaping idea.

3. CONTINUE LEARNING

Keep this in mind. You'll never arrive. You'll only continue *to refine*. World-shaping ideas are not fulfillable events. They're ever growing and expanding. You must do the same.

Too many leaders reach their pinnacles and feel no need to continue learning. They speak on their own words, read their own books, mentor others through their own thoughts.

Eventually they stagnate.

Think of your legacy like a Ferris Wheel. Your journey through this process has been to elevate you to the top of the ride. From the top, you can probably see a view few can visualize. With humility, it *can* continue for you indefinitely. Stop learning and put the focus back on yourself and the Ferris Wheel will start coming downward. Get too big for your own words and the Ferris Wheel will careen back to earth. Tragically, it's much harder to bring the Ferris Wheel back up once it reaches bottom.

Read more books *after* your world-shaping idea gains traction. You want to garner greater reference points through others' thoughts, and it should add to your metaphorical repertoire. Plus, it keeps your mind fresh and active. Remember, inspiration can lead you to just the right book, study, or lecture for your precise need at that time. Be as much of a sponge of knowledge and wisdom now as you were when attempting to find your world-shaping idea.

4. NEVER FORGET "THE ONE"

As you continue to elevate, your crowds may increase, the status of your followers may expand, the price of your speaking engagements may skyrocket. You may go from rooms of ten to halls of thousands, but "the one" is the person (or persons) in front of you at any given moment. That can be the star-struck fan whose life as a pizza delivery boy was altered from reading or listening to your thoughts. It could be the president of a nation. It might be the executive team at a Fortune 500 company. Treat them all equally. Learn from all of them.

The pizza boy may say something to you that changes the very scope of your mission. Don't miss it because you think he is beneath you.

I know it appears in this moment that this won't happen to you, but I've watched leader after leader discount conversations because they felt "the one" in front of them was "too small" for their newfound status.

Never give "beautiful people" more time and attention than others either. This is a trap of Ego and can lead to damaging repercussions on your reputation later. Single or not, never flirt. Always inspire. Think of every interaction as an opportunity to grow your world-shaping idea and add life and vitality to "the one" in front of you. That's why you started this journey in the first place, remember?

5. KEEP EGO IN CHECK

At nearly the beginning of this book, I personified and dissected Ego. Ego will always be in the way, at every step in this process. It will work to destroy your ability to present your world-shaping idea. If it can't destroy the idea, it will go after you personally. As you elevate, Ego will evolve and mature. It's hard to stay humble among constant praise and adoration, but you must.

Through every step, practice humility and meekness. Meekness is not weakness. It's tempered strength. Continue to grow *stronger* through this process, but keep grounded always.

Remember that giving in to Ego will only feel good for a nanosecond. You'll have your whole life to live with the rest of the regret. Don't let Ego affix an asterisk to your contribution to history.

HOW BIG WILL YOUR "WORLD" BECOME?

The subtitle of this book, and the goal of this journey, is for you to become a *world-shaper*. I just can't say how big your "world" will become. For some, your "world" may just be your family or your personal sphere of relationships. For others, it may be global. I've written the book to help with global awareness, but don't get discouraged if your "world" doesn't reach that status. Remember, that for those you do touch, you'll have changed *their world*.

LAST THOUGHTS

I wrote this book because I believe in this idea of personal world-shaping. I also believe in you, especially as you grow in the disciplines found in this book. Maybe it will spawn one world-shaper or maybe it will unleash thousands. It doesn't matter, as long as there are those in the world who are unleashed from turmoil, enlightened to a better future, and exposed to strategies that stifle human potential, I will have done my job. My writing will have been worth the trouble.

MLK2.0

There's no greater reward than to hear someone say, "You changed my life." As you develop into a world-shaper, I hope it becomes your greatest reward as well. I believe that MLK will smile down on you as you develop into an MLK2.0 and proudly, but humbly, broadcast your world-shaping idea.

EPILOGUE
SPARKS

(Springboarding off some of my world-shaping ideas)

I wrote this epilogue to give you some potential world-shaping ideas to springboard from. I've spoken these ideas to many leaders across a broad scope of domains and have been successful at changing paradigms in hearts and minds through them.

Some of these ideas are in the process of being developed into short films, books, or mini e-books. Feel free to begin to research these ideas on your own or develop your own ideas based on what's shared here. I encourage you to reach out to me at: david@purefusionmedia.com so we can dialog and strategize together in the future. I look forward to hearing your world-shaping thoughts as well!

SPARK 1: YOUR BODY IS FAR MORE OF AN INDEPENDENT ENTITY THAN YOU REALIZE

We operate our lives as if we're in control of our bodies. But as science has advanced, especially in the last ten years, it's discovered that our bodies are really autonomous machines. Let me give you a couple of examples:

Do you know why you contact a fever when you're sick? For centuries, science thought it was a *symptom* of an illness like a cold or a flu, but science has discovered it's not a symptom; it's an independent body reaction. Long before you grab the Nyquil or bury yourself under the bedsheets, your independent body recognizes that there's an offending virus or damaging agent in the body. The body, without you being the least bit aware, heats itself up while also causing the sweat glands to secrete in an effort to burn up the offending agent and remove it from the body. You discover you're sick long after your body has started fighting against it.

Moreover, when you're sick, you aren't really in control, are you? Though you may want to head to the beach or go see a movie perhaps, your body controls your actions until you're well again.

The preceding is a positive example of body control; the next example is not so optimistic.

When a person falls into nearly freezing water, rescuers realize they only have micro minutes to retrieve the individual from the frigid cold. Not simply because hypothermia sets in quickly, but also because of what the independent body does in that moment to survive. Whenever the body experiences that kind of dramatic decrease in temperature, the body realizes that death is eminent, so it protects the central component of a functioning body, the heart. Immediately, the body begins to draw all the blood in the individual back to the central region around the heart, to keep the heart pumping. In relocating the blood to the heart, the extremities, in this case the hands and feet, no longer function at capacity, and the person, despite his or her will to flail and stay afloat, becomes a human sinker weight.

Although you may not be fully aware of it, your body is, in essence, its own entity. As you give in to the urges of your body, your body exerts more and more control over your will. Pleasure, pride, greed, and lust, for example, don't just feel good to you; they feel great to your independent body, but the body is not simply focused on its selfish and independent desires holistically; the entire body operates *independent* of its other members. Each organ and facet of the body is selfishly independent of its other members.

For example, my brain and my taste buds crave fatty, greasy foods. Should I give in to these urges too often, my body begins to control my thoughts and body mechanics, stimulating me toward further stepping into gluttony, yet my heart and other organs can't handle the increase in food intake. My skin and soft tissue layers begin to suffer on account of what my brain and taste buds desire as well. What my taste buds and pleasure center in my brain continually desire wrecks havoc on the rest of my independent body, even leading to the death of the entire physiological system through heart attacks and pulmonary diseases like diabetes.

Many actions, especially those that produce addiction, allow the independent body to take control of the person. The body is an entity that doesn't have the capacity to know how to keep our best interests at heart. By engaging in Addiction-Producing Actions, the body then begins to take over the will and…

SPARK 2: ADDICTION IS THE MOMENT THAT THE WILL OF THE PERSON HAS BEEN COMPLETELY OVERTAKEN BY THE INDEPENDENT BODY OF THE PERSON.

Excerpt taken from my book, "Parables & Parallels")

No one who walks into a bar on a Friday night says, "Tonight I'm going to get addicted." No one who routinely plays blackjack with his or her friends on Monday evenings and watches World Championship Poker on satellite TV thinks, "Tonight gambling will start destroying my life." He or she simply continues doing the same thing he or she has done in the past. At the point of addiction, a different result occurs.

The first instance of addiction is much like the moment a gun finally goes off in a game of Russian roulette. The more times one plays, the greater the probability the gun will discharge. It's the repetition of Addiction-Producing Actions that provide the bullets to fill the gun's empty chambers. In this metaphor we discover the danger. While the potentially addicted individual may be the one holding the gun, the gun itself is the flesh (physical body) of the individual.

In other words, the individual (the will) does not determine when the gun goes off; his or her independent physical body does.

The individual who repeatedly pulls the trigger only to have the gun continually misfire naively concludes, *I'm in control here*. In reality, bullets are being added to the gun without the individual being the least bit aware. The gun goes off when the independent body, not the will, decides it's time to fire. All the individual can do prior to the moment of addictive discharge is walk away from the gun. He or she can't begin the game and control the result.

Unfortunately, leaving the tabl, even prior to

addiction, is harder than one might think.

Keeping with the Russian roulette metaphor, neuroscience and genetics have uncovered two important aspects of this addictive game. First, geneticists have determined that planted in the genes of each individual is the predisposition for certain addiction-producing actions. England, for example, is considering the analysis of young children's DNA to determine if they have a propensity toward addictive drugs such as heroin or cocaine. Secular scientists use these genetic predisposition discoveries to legitimize and rationalize certain behaviors. As secular science uncovers these objective discoveries, its ambassadors erroneously conclude that these actions are simply part of the evolutionary genetic makeup of the human animal. To reinterpret a quote from *The Matrix*: To deny one's genetic impulses *is to deny being human.*

Bringing these discoveries back to our metaphorical game of Russian roulette, we uncover that addiction is not played on a single table. Addiction is birthed out of a number of different repetitious actions. There are a myriad of tables on which an individual can begin to play, ranging from drugs to pornography, from violence to gambling, and a plethora of other actions. For each individual, certain guns already are loaded on the table before he begins to play. The guns of drugs and sex may be half full of bullets for one person, while another's loaded gun may be overeating, and another's, child molestation. All the enemy of mankind need do is make sure the right game is well-disguised and enjoyable enough to play so that the individual steps to the table with the right gun (or guns) for his or her genetic predisposition and sits down at the table.

Through clever marketing tactics, progressive ideologies, and mammoth financial capital, not only do these addictive games surround us, but also nearly all tables (all of the Addiction-Producing Actions correlating to mankind's genetic predispositions) are now open and available to play. Even worse, the path to one's addiction table and its preloaded weapons can merely be the click of the mouse or the turning on of a smart phone or tablet.

Through revelations in neuroscience, we learn that the game is further fixed. At the moment of any action, the human brain builds up and develops synapses corresponding to that particular course of action. Whether it's the opening of a door, the smelling of a flower, or the feeling of feet hitting the pavement during a run, synaptic pathways are produced. The more intense the action or event, the greater the synaptic buildup (and release of neurochemicals) occurs. Once a pathway tied to a certain course of action has been built, the brain's natural inclination is further travel down that pathway. The more one continues in that action, the greater the infrastructure is strengthened to that neuronal pathway and the more difficult it's to deviate from that course of action.

For example, at the moment of sexual ejaculation, the brain is flooded with the neurotransmitters dopamine and serotonin. Sex doesn't just feel good to the person; it feels great to the brain and correspondingly to the body. Dopamine and serotonin travel across the neurological paths built from the actions leading up to that moment, as well as from the strongest additional pathways. The brain then knows to feel this good again, the same course of action should be taken. At this moment of neuronal and physical ecstasy (ejaculation), the will already enters the first phases of being subjugated by the flesh. Once addictive actions are no longer enjoyable to the individual (through his will), the body and brain will still desire and fight for the same effect. Long before the actual physical addiction, or the moment the gun finally goes off, the brain itself already has made it difficult for the individual to leave the table.

Both before *and* after addiction occurs, the will of the man is still being perpetually dominated by the independent body of the same man.

Though it's not claimed as such, addiction treatment centers are not curing people of addiction. They're attempting to win the battle over the body of the individual that has wholly dominated the will of the individual. The person isn't freed of addiction; his or her independent body is once again controlled and restricted, as it should have been in the first place. During the process leading to addiction, science unveils that the flesh gains further and further dominance. What are the secular world's best responses to its own scientific discoveries?

One of science's current solutions is to produce pharmaceutical products; in essence, to introduce poisons into the body that reduce the power of the flesh so persons can enjoy addiction-producing actions longer without the same addictive result. Science is poisoning the body instead of recognizing and dealing with the realities of these addiction-producing actions that they themselves have discovered through their own disciplines! These pharmacological solutions come affixed with a massive list of new objective and detrimental physiological consequences. These consequences are stamped on the front of plastic bottles right after the phrase "side effects include." In many instances these side effects are more destructive to the physiology of the individual than the result of the initial action.

Worse, there are plans by some genetic experts and medical institutions to extract DNA samples of embryonic human life prior to birth. The thinking is that parents can be warned of potentially addictive future behavior patterns should they decide to terminate the pregnancy. I already have spoken of the consideration in England to test for genetic predispositions for heroin and cocaine in the young.

What does science want to do with children who have the genetic propensity? Inject them with these narcotic drugs as children so that as adults, they no longer desire the pursuit of what they've already been given. The bottom line is that the three best secular solutions to this objective game of Russian roulette are poison, early forced addiction, and death. For the sake of our society, we must demand better solutions.

SPARK 3: WANT TO SHAPE THE WORLD? FOCUS ON OUTCOMES, NOT ACTIONS.

(excerpt taken from my book, "CRE8TVE SUCCESS")

If there's one thing I wish I could skywrite over the entire face of the planet, it's this: **Subjective actions and declarations produce objective consequences.**

Imagine a man named John. John is the top performer in his small-sized marketing firm, a five-year-old startup with twenty employees. John is in his late twenties and is an above average looking man. His youthful vigor and attractive charm serve him well at his company. As a marketing stud, John fancies himself as a bit of womanizer, often bragging to his co-workers, "I can sleep with whoever I want; it's not really hurting anybody."

To John, his statement is true; he can sleep with whomever he wants without consequence, as long as the moments are consensual. While his declaration is subjective, there has been little objective repercussion, at least that he *knows* about.

Suppose John contracts a serious STD such as HIV that *one time* he wasn't careful enough. Now John's life faces radical changes.

First, he must deal with the psychological complications of his new condition. His countenance falls and his anxiety rises, knowing he's now a "marked man" in future intimate encounters.

Second, he must visit the local clinic two times a week to monitor his condition, which thankfully remains negative. Since the clinic is only open between eight am and six pm, he must leave the office during business hours at least once a week. The psychological pressure mounts, and John's performance at the office suffers. John's attitude and lack of focus causes the firm to lose one of its top clients, a company responsible for 23 percent of the firm's yearly revenue.

Left to deal with the financial aftermath, decisions must be made. Do they fire John? Absolutely not; John still manages more accounts than any other employee. Instead, the business fires two lower tier employees. The first employee was a man in his mid-forties. In addition to a first and second mortgage, the fired employee had a daughter about to enter college. The prestige of the collegiate institution she could attend was contingent on his salary, and the daughter is forced to go to a lower quality school academically. This causes years of financial and social repercussion on the daughter, while daddy defaults on his mortgage obligations.

The second employee, a younger male just out of college, didn't have to deal with critical financial decisions like paying a mortgage, but he did have a nine dollar a day latte habit at Starbucks. Unable to afford his java fix, Starbucks loses approximately $2,500 in yearly revenue. Add on a few more bad situations brought on by a few other Starbucks patrons and the local Starbucks lets one of its baristas go to cover the expenses, leaving the barista to suffer the aftermath.

Back to John's company one more time. John never really shakes off the anxiety and depression, and more clients travel elsewhere, taking that essential revenue with them. Eventually the company fires John. A year later the company folds, the employees scatter, and the founders are left carting a quarter of a million dollars of debt. John's womanizing declaration had real and powerful consequence when the subjectivity of his verbal statement clashed with the objectivity of the real world.

Notice that the outcome started with John, but traveled quickly and effortlessly, like a virus, into the surrounding landscape. Situations like John's happen around us ubiquitously; we just rarely connect the dots. As Jack Johnson brilliantly penned,

"…Wanna take a time lapse and look at it backwards."

Connecting dots often begins by tracing them back to their sources.

You might think I'm a bit extreme here, but consider the power of this understanding. I have a good friend who's a private practice physician. He believes that diseases such as diabetes are not merely a biologic complication; they're strategic conduits. The *intent* of diabetes is to destroy the body. It's not that diabetes *inadvertently* causes body destruction. Diabetes needs a driver, and that driver is poor diet, lack of exercise, etc.

My doctor friend sits with his patients and asks them to imagine a predatory animal such as a lion or bear. He then asks his patient, "If that lion could attack you, what would happen?" The patient naturally declares that the lion would most likely destroy your flesh and consume your body parts: your eyes, stomach, heart, etc. He explains that diabetes is like a lion; it *craves* to destroy you. The more you engage poor dieting and lack of exercise, the more powerful the lion can become.

His insights have brought him to speak to hundreds of doctors at conferences, and he's changing how physicians see disease, not as complications or outcomes, but as deliberate strategies.

Years ago, I sat down with the nanaging director of the neurology center at one of the top universities in the country. I presented him with a five page paper on my findings in neuroscience, and specifically how neuroplasticity, addiction, and certain seemingly "fundamental" moral declarations played out strategically. I took three seemingly disparate findings and connected dots.

A few days later he called my office, asserting, "I don't know how you know my field at this level, but these are more profound insights than any of my neuroscientists and neurosurgeons have previously presented. After years of scientific study and the latest in technological advancement, the best we've been able to do is to pump people full of drugs or cut them. You're telling me there's a third way, and I believe it." We were negotiating a day of talks with his team to discuss these insights, but the economy collapsed in 2008 and unfortunately the moment passed.

I have another friend who started a non-profit centered around government and law enforcement partnerships to turn the tide on human trafficking. As we sat and discussed his business formulation, I told him, "If you want to address human trafficking, you need to go back to one of the main sources: *internet pornography*." I didn't make this declaration because of the "moral" implications of porn. The declaration was founded in the objective neurological complications attached to the looking at porn, in private, in massive quantities, with little societal repercussion. I wrote a forty page ebook entitled *Addiction's Tipping Point* elucidating how and why addictions are tipping in our society, not because of "sinful behavior" as a moralist might purport, but instead I focused on the physiological, philosophical, and technological evolution of our postmodern and secularized society.

Humanity suffers from disease, divorce, depression, despair, ad infinitum, not simply due to our subjective actions, but also because of *the objective consequence* of our subjective actions. Those consequences weigh heavily on society, both individually and collectively.

Connecting dots requires us to drown out the surface noise of peoples' declarations and focus on the outcomes that occur, both to the individual and to the society at large. Empathy cares for the individual beyond his or her personal desires. It sees the big picture, past, present, and future. Apathy encourages people to continue down damaging pathways unhindered, blinded or callous to the objective consequence lying just beyond their subjective declarations.

SPARK 4: HEY CHURCH! START ASKING THE WHY QUESTIONS!

(excerpt taken from a recent podcast)

As a Christian, I wish the church would start asking the "why" questions.

For many years, the church has primarily been based on the "God said it, I believe it, and that settles it" mantra. While it appears to resemble faith, it's incredibly hollow and lacks any ability to penetrate the culture at large.

Suppose you have a three or four-year-old daughter. One day, as you're cooking some pasta on the stove, she ventures into the kitchen and reaches out to grab the pot. In that moment, you reach down, grab her hand firmly, and say, "Don't touch the stove!" Now, you've given her a rather dogmatic command. I mean it started with Do Not! right? Is your intent to restrict her from the kitchen and the stove because of your selfish and self-centered desires? No, it's the exact opposite; you don't want her to get burned! You aren't thinking about yourself; you're thinking about your daughter, or better yet, you're thinking about your daughter's protection.

So hopefully, around the age of nine or ten, you're going to take her into the kitchen and show her how to carefully use the stove and reveal to her the joys of cooking. Maybe she becomes a chef someday, who knows, but your dogmatic "do not touch" command was never for her restriction.

Now, imagine never having that talk with your daughter. At age forty, she's still afraid to go near the stove because all her life, "daddy at the age of three told her not to," and for four decades she obeyed you out of love for her dad. Are you a good father? No, quite frankly *you're an idiot.*

Sadly, I think that in many cases that's how the church sees God's commands and words. I don't need to know why; I simply need to know that "Daddy said not too."

Bible-understanding Christians have the answers to the world's problems, issues, and struggles. God wants us to share His heart with the world. To understand his heart is to understand the why's behind his commands. The why's of God's commands come down to the liberation, protection, and powerful intention of God's greatest creation: humanity. Once we begin to shift the focus of God's heart back onto people's bodies, minds families, and futures – as well as their souls, we'll begin to not only take our place as influencers and culture shapers, but I believe we'll reconnect to the heart of God.

We've got to stop being like the forty-year-old, saying, "Don't touch the stove, because my Daddy said not to." It's not going to work in our society today. Here's the point; the world may not want to adhere to God's statements that appear to restrict actions, but they're desperate to be healed from the damaging outcomes of their actions, such as disease, depression, and depravity.

For now, we've to begin to search out the "why" behind God's commands and open ourselves up to the joys that follow because that's what God always intended.

How do we do that? We've to learn to transplant scripture from theology and into our modern-day world, infusing the words of God with the *world of God*. The facts are all around us. My favorite singer songwriter Jack Johnson wrote:

"There's puzzle pieces in the ground, but nobody seems to be digging."

Traffic in the Sky

As Christians in this culture, we need to start digging, we need to start recognizing and understanding not just "that" God said something, but "why" he said it. That "why" will be serving you coffee this morning or working in the cubicle next to you or busily pushing past you on the street. It doesn't matter what they believe, what actions they commit, or what political stances they may have, they're all part of the answer to the why questions.

Live inspired.

www.ingramcontent.com/pod-product-compliance
Lightning Source LLC
LaVergne TN
LVHW051118080426
835510LV00018B/2101